'This is an outstanding book that is hugely engaging, deeply challenging, brilliantly creative and extremely practical. I have no doubt that, if a generation were to take the contents of this book seriously, we would see not only a nation but a world transformed.'
Laura Hancock, National Ministries Director, Youth for Christ

T0327288

Neil O'Boyle is the National Director of British Youth for Christ. He has been involved in youth work for over 25 years, has lived in multiple countries and visited over 80 nations with the ministry of Youth for Christ. He loves Lego, *Star Wars*, Leeds United, hiking, mountains, his wife, his four children – and God.

NEIL
O'BOYLE

UNDER CONSTRUCTION

WORKING WITH THE ARCHITECT

spck

YOUTH
FOR CHRIST

First published in Great Britain in 2019

Society for Promoting Christian Knowledge
36 Causton Street
London SW1P 4ST
www.spck.org.uk

The author and publisher have made every effort to ensure that the external website and
email addresses included in this book are correct and up to date at the time of going to
press. The author and publisher are not responsible for the content, quality or continuing
accessibility of the sites.

Scripture quotations marked GNB are taken from the Good News Bible published by The
Bible Societies/HarperCollins Publishers Ltd UK and are copyright © American Bible
Society, 1966, 1971, 1976, 1992, 1994.

Quotations marked NASB are taken from the NEW AMERICAN STANDARD BIBLE®,
Copyright © 1960, 1962, 1963, 1968, 1971, 1972, 1973, 1975, 1977, 1995 by The Lockman
Foundation. Used by permission.

Quotations marked NIV are taken from The Holy Bible, New International Version
(Anglicized edition). Copyright © 1979, 1984, 2011 by Biblica. Used by permission of
Hodder & Stoughton Ltd, an Hachette UK company. All rights reserved. 'NIV' is a registered
trademark of Biblica. UK trademark number 1448790.

Quotations marked NLT are taken from the Holy Bible, New Living Translation, copyright ©
1996. Used by permission of Tyndale House Publishers, Inc., Carol Stream, Illinois 60189,
USA. All rights reserved.

Quotations marked WEB are taken from The World English Bible (WEB), a public domain
(no copyright) modern English translation of the Holy Bible, based on the American
Standard Version of the Holy Bible first published in 1901, the Biblia Hebraica Stutgartensa
Old Testament, and the Greek Majority Text New Testament.

Every effort has been made to seek permission to use copyright material reproduced in
this book. The publisher apologizes for those cases where permission might not have been
sought and, if notified, will formally seek permission at the earliest opportunity.

British Library Cataloguing-in-Publication Data
A catalogue record for this book is available from the British Library

ISBN 978-0-281-08207-0
eBook ISBN 978-0-281-08208-7

1 3 5 7 9 10 8 6 4 2

Typeset by Fakenham Prepress Solutions, Fakenham, Norfolk NR21 8NL
Printed in Great Britain by Jellyfish Print Solutions

eBook by Fakenham Prepress Solutions, Fakenham, Norfolk NR21 8NL

Produced on paper from sustainable forests

Contents

Foreword

I don't think we are called to be ordinary or mundane as people who follow Jesus! I believe that we need to keep our gaze fixed on Jesus – walking him, trusting him and living him. And yielding our whole life to the Holy Spirit, who will transform us into Christlikeness.

Why would you ever want to be ordinary, or to live a life which is not abundant? Jesus Christ invites us on a journey, a journey that transforms us into the people we were created to be, wonderfully redeemed by Jesus Christ.

What I like about this book is that it doesn't settle for the ordinary but invites the reader to allow Jesus Christ to wander the corridors of our lives and examine any room that might be off limits. There are three simple outcomes – freedom, life and transformation; and one simple purpose – a closer relationship with Jesus Christ.

Don't settle for the average in your relationship with the Lord or the way you behave; rather, let the Holy Spirit get to work. He is interested in one very big thing: you! So turn your focus on him. Let him work in and through you. May you become more and more like Jesus Christ. After all, what else matters?

John Sentamu
Archbishop of York

Introduction

Do you ever make mistakes, get frustrated, lose your rag or feel jealous? Do you like your own space and want to do your own thing? Are you nice one moment and grumpy the next? Are you consumed by your needs and who you are? If that doesn't describe you, it sadly describes me.

There was this guy a long time ago who wrote a book that caught my imagination. It was called *My Heart, Christ's Home*. It asked the question, 'What would it look like for Jesus to make his home inside our lives?'

I have been a Christian for around 30 years. If my life resembles a house, then there is still major renovation work needed to make it a really great place to live. From the outside I look like a pretty okay person, but on the inside there is damp coming through the walls and the banister is falling off, the shower has a leak and the windows let in draughts. In other words, there is room for improvement.

Jesus is not remotely intimidated; he is ready to get to work. What's more, he isn't merely visiting while he makes the changes; he is moving in.

I don't want to be an okay Christian. I want to be the very best person that God designed me to be, who lives the life that God has called me to live and where nothing holds me back.

How about you?

Get ready for a dangerously awesome read that offers hope and encouragement but also asks the hard questions – which implies some tough actions.

This is a book based on your life, pictured as a house, and Jesus is asking for total access!

In the first five chapters Jesus will inspect the building, examine the floorboards, look for cracks in the walls, see how much light gets into the house and check the roof for leaks. Once that all looks okay, Jesus will want to move freely around every room in your life. So in Chapters 5–11 he will visit the living room, dining room, study, kitchen, bathroom and bedroom. He is keen to explore with you exactly what goes on and what you get up to in those rooms. Finally, in Chapter 12, he will turn his attention to the garden and set to work on what grows there so that the world will see its beauty and share its fruits.

Giving Jesus access means allowing change to happen. While I might not be perfect, I am a better person than I was a year ago, and the person I was a year ago was a much better person than five years before that, and so on. God is in the business of renovation. There are quick fixes and there are long-term projects. Our part in all of this is to give him permission to start the transformation project. He knows exactly who you are and who you can become. This is going to be a life-changing, life-defining experience provided you are willing to hand over the keys.

Turn the page to start the journey!

1 RENOVATE

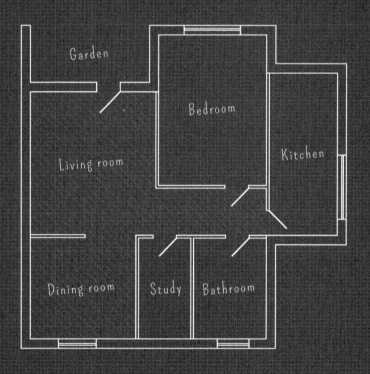

'What if this is as good as it gets?'

That was my opening line to a room packed full of teenagers on the last night of a Christian festival. My point was that every year their parents made them attend the festival (because they were at the adult version) and every year they were challenged to live passionately for God, going home ready to give their faith a chance. However, within a few weeks, most of them would return to their old habits and routines, and their faith would take a back seat, until the next compulsory festival came around.

What if that is as good as the Christian experience gets? Struggle, temptation, guilt, followed by the annual reset at the big Christian festival, and then comes struggle, temptation, guilt, annual reset, and on it goes.

God has so much more for us than that! When Jesus said, 'I have come in order that you might have life – life in all its fullness' (John 10.10, GNB), I don't think he had in mind a cycle of defeats and resets. There definitely are challenges, difficulties and discouragements along the way, but many of us are yet to figure out the life God has for us.

At the end of the road where I grew up was an old derelict house. Parts of the roof had caved in and nailed wooden panels covered the windows and doors to prevent trespassers. My parents hated the very sight of the house, hoping it would be bulldozed. My brother told me an old man had been killed in that house and his spirit tormented anyone who dared to go inside. As a 10-year-old boy, there was obviously only one thing to do – break in!

3

IS YOUR EXPERIENCE OF THE CHRISTIAN LIFE AS GOOD AS IT GETS?

In broad daylight, on one particular summer's day, my brother and I crept up to the door, pulled two panels off and squeezed between the gap. We were inside.

It was dark, but streaks of light shone through the boarded-up window panels and parts of the missing roof. The floorboards were broken, the walls crumbling and the stairs creaked as we headed to the first floor. My heart was beating so hard I thought my brother might have heard it, and if not him then the ghost of the murdered old man must surely have sensed my fear.

On the first floor, in what must have been the former owner's bedroom, there was no sight nor sound of a tormenting spirit. We stood in silence. My brother eventually started to call him, 'Come out, old man; we are here in your house!' No response. And then 'BOOM!'

I jumped in terror and ran for the stairs. I couldn't get out quick enough. My brother was shouting, 'Come on, let's get out . . . it's coming!' I was at the door – I was struggling to get through the gap we had created. 'Get out!' my brother shrieked.

I eventually rolled through and ended up in a ball on the floor outside. I started to get up. My brother was now through, but he was laughing!

'What?' I asked, confused, scrambling to my feet.

'You should have seen your face when I went "Boom"!'

Reality began to dawn on me, and fear started quickly to give way to anger. My brother had orchestrated the whole thing. There was no old man.

That house had been neglected and needed serious renovation. It needed an owner who would love it and invest in repairing it – to restore it not to its former self, but to something even greater. Eventually someone bought that old house and did exactly that. It received more than tender loving care; it received a substantial investment.

Very recently, I bought my own house. Within a short period of time, the roof developed a leak and we faced a hefty bill to get it fixed. Being the owner, and wanting to keep the house in good order, I had little choice but to fix it. I now have a watertight new roof.

What if our lives were compared to a house? Can you say your house is in perfect order and everything works the way it should, and looks impeccable to visitors? Or, if we are truthful, are there a few problems such as the roof or the plumbing, and might the viewing of some rooms be off limits to guests? Lots of people live with issues of shame that they lock away, hidden out of sight; others struggle about comparisons – perhaps the house is too small, with little value? Some might fear ridicule over the limited possibilities that their house might have, a lack of potential perhaps, and some may just be embarrassed that the house has not had much care, losing its shape or its appearance. Whatever the issues, you might feel that your house is not perfect and you desire its transformation. But for whatever reason, that seems most unlikely to happen. Do you need an architect or a miracle worker? Are the floorboards corroding – which can easily be fixed – or are the walls beginning to lean, with large ugly cracks developing, making the house potentially dangerous?

What if the original designer or architect of your home wanted to pay a visit? He or she wants to come by and see how the house looks today – if it is in good condition, and whether there have

BUILD A HOUSE
USING THIS GRID.

been any modifications and improvements. How would you feel? While I have never had an architect ask to make an inspection, for years we have lived in rented accommodation, which meant the house was not ours, and once or twice a year the owner would turn up and check whether we were taking care of his or her property. Sometimes the visit went well. Sometimes the owner felt we had not cared for the house properly.

What state is your metaphorical house in today? Being a Christian means I see the world in a certain way. For example, I believe that you were made by God (the Master Architect): not as an accident – the Bible says God knew your name before the beginning of time; nor as an experiment – the Bible also says that God knit you together in your mother's womb and you were wonderfully made. Somewhere along the way, that which God has made has taken its fair share of wear and tear, and things are not quite as they were designed to be.

Let me tell you my story. I struggled at school; I had concentration challenges, so paid no attention, and my grades indicated I had the intelligence of a goldfish. I was an introvert and so wasn't socially outgoing. I was small and not overly strong, and I was of average appearance. I certainly wasn't a strong A in any area of my life – more like a consistent D across the board.

My lack of confidence resulted in a bunch of poor choices and, to cut a very long story short, those choices had a serious impact on my overall well-being. On New Year's Eve, at the age of 16, I found myself locked up in a hospital unit. It was the kind that had bars outside my window. My choices had left me anxious, depressed and suicidal. My 'house' was crumbling and I certainly didn't want guests: any attention was embarrassing. In reality I had failed to pay the mortgage and the bank was taking ownership of my property. I had lost control.

After what felt like an eternity I was eventually released, though to be honest I didn't feel any better. I gained an increased fear of social settings and didn't want to go outside. I had lost all of my friends, which at this stage in life suited me fine. I had an old classmate who had heard my story and must have felt sorry for me because he kept calling and wanted to meet up.

By this point I couldn't even answer the door or pick up the phone. My mum became so frustrated that she insisted I speak to Mark (my classmate) and I eventually forced myself to speak on the phone. He said that he wanted to take me out, and if I agreed to go once he would leave me alone in future. That seemed like a great offer. I weighed up my fear of going outside with his promise to back off, and accepted the terms. I stupidly did not ask where we were going.

He picked me up, and to this day I can remember feeling over-whelmed as I left the house after weeks of being inside. We drove to the nearby town and pulled up outside what appeared to be a church. I followed him into the hall and immediately wanted to turn around. The hall must have had over 200 young people. It felt as if everyone was looking at me (I later discovered they were, as Mark had asked them to pray for me, and they were surprised I had turned up).

I was at some weird church event called Youth for Christ. Was this some kind of cult? A band started to play trendy Christian songs and everyone joined in. It felt as if I was witnessing a freak show. These creepy Christians seemed unusually ecstatic, and I couldn't help but wonder if they were paid to smile like that. Nobody could be that happy!

I had had enough. I needed to get out. I was starting to have a panic attack around these weirdos. At that moment the band stopped playing and everyone sat down. I was now the only one standing, so, feeling awkward, I took a seat. At this point a young woman got up to speak, but I quickly zoned out and didn't listen to a word of what she said.

I zoned back in for her last sentence. 'If you are here tonight and you do not know Jesus as your Lord and Saviour then you can do so and give him your life!' Absolutely nothing about that statement made any sense. 'Lord and Saviour' and 'give him my life'? What did she mean? Who taught her to talk like that?

Something stirred within me like a washing machine on full spin, and I found myself praying, 'Okay, God, I don't know if you even exist, but if you do then you can take my stupid pathetic life, because if you don't, I will!'

A moment passed, and then I realized I had just done something I should have thought through, because whoever God might be, I became increasingly aware that there was a very good chance he had just heard me. I started to feel different: I felt a sense of inexplicable peace. I then felt as if electricity was going through my body on a voltage that seemed high enough to fry me. Everything around me began to disappear and I felt I was in the presence of something much greater than myself or anything else I had ever encountered. I had a suspicion I had caught God's attention, crazy as that might seem.

I left that building that night feeling totally different. My fear had completely subsided and I had a profound sense of hope. I felt as though the God of the universe had personally reached out and made contact.

Since that night I have never looked back and I have never been the same again. Jesus said, 'I have come to heal the broken hearted, set the captives free and release the oppressed' (Luke 4.18, my version). I was different; that was all I could say. I had no words for what had happened.

If my life was a house, the original architect had not just paid it a visit, he had moved in!

In the Bible Jesus said, 'I stand at the door and knock. Whoever opens the door I will come in and eat with them' (Rev. 3.20, my version). Jesus himself refers to our lives as a house, but the door is closed to him. He may knock, but only we can open it. The Bible also says that Jesus makes his home in the hearts of his followers. When you become a Christian, Jesus moves in, but before he starts making changes, he waits for you to give him permission. Too many Christians leave Jesus in the hallway of their lives.

Jesus the architect started a lifelong renovation project on my 16-year-old self. There is not a day that goes by without his handiwork or craftsmanship making tweaks and alterations, seeking continual improvements. Sometimes those improvements involve a stripping back.

There is no house too ugly, broken or beyond repair. The door may be hanging off its hinges, the roof shot or half a wall gone, but once he moves in, the architect will start to see new potential and opportunities for alterations and transformation. He is simply waiting for the freedom to move around and make changes.

To be a Christian means that we are making a decision to live for him, to become more like him and to be in a lifelong relationship with

SOME CHANGES?

BIG
CHANGES?

MINOR
CHANGES?

NO
CHANGES?

him. Old habits come under scrutiny, but Jesus is about freedom and transformation.

Before you read any further, take a moment to think about a couple of questions:

1 If your life is a house, are there things in it that need attention?
2 Will you allow God to work out what might need doing?

Question 2 should not be answered lightly. In my case, and in the case of many other people who said yes and gave him the freedom to move around, our lives have never been the same again.

Change is inevitable, but only if you agree to the architect's terms. Let's close this chapter by reflecting on one thing. If God did make us and wants to connect with us, then might it be logical to expect that our lives will never be entirely right until he features significantly within them? We can't leave Jesus in the corridor. He wants the freedom to move around and make changes. What does that mean? It means that whatever you are currently experiencing, it is not as good as it gets.

God has so much more in store. Allow him to move around your life, give him the keys to every door and hand control over to him.

You were made for a purpose. You were made for so much more.

REFLECT:

IS YOUR FAITH CAUGHT IN A CYCLE OF STRUGGLES, TEMPTATION, GUILT AND RESET?

DO YOU OFTEN WONDER, 'IS THIS AS GOOD AS IT GETS?' OR, 'IS THERE MORE TO BEING A CHRISTIAN THAN THIS?'

HAVE YOU LEFT JESUS IN THE HALLWAY OF YOUR LIFE? IS HE FREE TO ROAM AROUND, OR ARE THERE ROOMS OFF LIMITS?

MEDITATE:

AND I PRAY THAT **CHRIST** WILL MAKE HIS **HOME** MORE AND MORE **IN YOUR LIFE.**

(EPH. 3.17, MY VERSION)

ACT:

IF YOU ARE WILLING, GIVE JESUS FULL ACCESS TO EVERY AREA OF YOUR LIFE BY PRAYING THIS PRAYER:

LORD JESUS, THANK YOU THAT YOU LOVE ME AND LIVE IN ME. TODAY I GIVE YOU FULL ACCESS TO EVERY AREA OF MY LIFE. DO AS YOU WILL. CHANGE ME ACCORDING TO YOUR DESIRES AND DRAW ME CLOSER TO YOU!

MAKE A NOTE BY WRITING DOWN TODAY'S DATE AND INDICATE THAT YOU HAVE GIVEN JESUS COMPLETE FREEDOM TO RENOVATE YOUR LIFE.

2 FLOORBOARDS

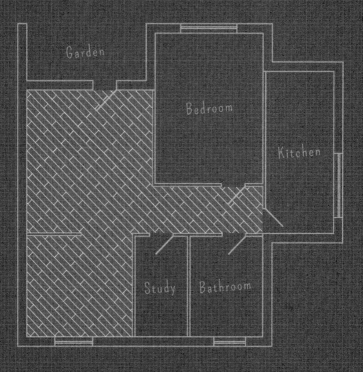

This is going to sound slightly strange, but just bear with me.

A few years back I was praying for a woman. She was a complete stranger at church but she asked if I would pray for her. She didn't tell me why, so I didn't have much to go on.

As I started to pray, a clear and very vivid picture of a house came to my mind, but the house did not have any floorboards. I was struck by the fact that if you were to walk through the front door you would fall into an ugly ditch. The frame to the building was fine but no one could live properly in this particular house, as there was no floor.

I shared my picture and felt slightly awkward in doing so. Part way through sharing I noticed that the woman was reacting to what I was saying. At the end I asked her if she was okay. She replied, 'I have had the same dream over and over again, as if it were on repeat, for the last week. It was a house without any floorboards, just like the picture you shared. I don't know what it means!'

Jesus told a story of two people who built a house. The first person built his house on the beach. Its foundation was made of sand. When the storms came, the house broke up and could not stand, because it had no real foundations. Shifting sands do not act as a great support. The second man built his house on a rock. When the storms came, his foundation was solid and the house remained standing.

A house without any floorboards or a concrete base would be pretty hard to live in. You couldn't set any of your furniture in place, or walk from one room to another. A house needs the basics of solid floors. Without them you are in trouble.

Now, while that might seem logical, plenty of people live their lives without floorboards! You might be surprised to discover you could be one of them.

I once lived in America. One day, I received an urgent call from a local Youth for Christ team asking if I would be available to go to the local high school where they wanted me to sit on a panel and answer questions from a group of teenagers and parents who were feeling pretty confused and upset. I agreed, but only after I agreed did I ask for details. Apparently a student had just ended his life and it was the fourth suicide in less than three years in that particular school.

The panel consisted of a counsellor, a theologian, a pastor and myself (I felt very inferior). The crowd were asking some tough questions.

Eventually a question came my way: 'Why did he kill himself and why was he so selfish?' I had no idea, and my mind had gone blank.

I took a moment, then replied, 'I don't know why he killed himself, but I don't think he was selfish. You see, to get to a place where you are thinking of ending your life usually means you are suffering from depression, and depression is the absence of hope. When you have no hope, it feels as if you have no good options, and when you have no good options you can make really poor choices. It doesn't, however, make it right. Depression is a battle and it has to be fought. You have to just keep pushing through it, no matter how hard it gets, and keep trying to move forward.'

I sat down and began to reflect on my answer, fearing that what I had said had been terribly unhelpful.

Then a note was passed to me from the crowd. I took it, opened it and realized I had been handed what was most likely a suicide note. It only had four words on it. The note read, in scrawled hand-writing, 'I've lost the war.' I had talked about a battle and someone had replied, 'Forget the battle. I've lost the war!'

My heart began to race. I jumped to my feet and asked for the microphone. Words began to pour out of my mouth.

'Listen. I just got a note. I don't know who sent it and I don't know what is going on in your life, but I do know this: you haven't lost the war. The reason I know is because you are still here, you are still in the battle, and there is a battle to fight. What's more we want to fight with you, so let us help you. And even more importantly, God says in the Bible that he wants to fight for you. You need to give him a chance to do that. Please, whoever you are, come and see us afterwards.'

I sat back down and began to tremble. I was terrified I hadn't done a good enough job. What if the person didn't respond? The night soon ended and people began to leave. I remained sitting on my stool at the front, just waiting. After a while, when almost everyone had gone, I realized nobody was coming forward. I got off the stool and collected my bag.

As I was heading for the door, I was pulled over by a member of the team. 'Neil, let me introduce you to Angie.' I turned to see a 16- or 17-year-old girl who looked as though she had been crying. The leader explained Angie's story. She had been battling with depression and suicidal thoughts for some time and was now feeling pretty desperate. Angie admitted to writing the note.

That night we prayed for Angie, talked to her parents and made sure she received professional help.

THE LORD WILL
**FIGHT
FOR YOU;**
YOU NEED ONLY
**TO BE
STILL.**

(EXOD. 14.14, NIV)

HOW MIGHT GOD FIGHT FOR YOU?

A few months later I was at the airport, leaving the USA to return to live in the UK. As I waited for my flight, Angie popped into my mind and I sent a text asking how she was doing. Just as my gate was called, I had a little bing on my phone. 'Angie is doing great in her mental health and even better in her spiritual walk with God.' Angie's life had turned a significant corner.

What Angie needed more than anything else in her life was hope!

Too many people simply exist without any sense of hope. The very first thing Jesus does when he walks into your house, your life, is to lay an entire new foundation. Whether your floorboards are broken, entirely gone or seem okay to you, he will pull them up and lay fresh new floorboards that have hope as a foundation to everything.

- Do you matter? Yes.
- Is there a reason for your existence beyond science? Yes.
- Is there more to life than routine? Yes.
- Is there a way through the most horrific of situations? Yes.
- Is there something after death? Yes.

There is hope, there is truth, there is more. You were created for so much more.

So let me ask you, if I may, what is the foundation of your house (life) built upon?

For some, it is the pursuit of excellence. Be the best, do the best you can and have the best of everything; don't settle for anything less. For others, it's love, and relationships are key. For some it's the pursuit of satisfaction, whatever that means and however it may be found. For most, it's existence: I need to get through today and move a little further forward on the journey of life. Which is fine, until something gets in the way.

What happens if you are not the best, or you lose someone you love, or the satisfaction buzz runs out, or the journey of existence turns out to be boring or, you suddenly realize, only temporary? What do you do then? Everything your life is built upon is suddenly in question.

When Jesus lays the foundations, we are building our very lives upon him. He now is the one that matters, he is the one we trust, he is the one we can rely on and he is the one who gives us meaning and purpose. He shapes our values and the way that we think. He calls us into relationship with him and from that relationship everything else flows. When things go wrong, we don't need to panic – he becomes our source of confidence. Life is no longer built upon our achievements but his. And what has he achieved? Life as we know it – and a universe far beyond what any star-gazer can see. I would rather place my confidence in God than in my own abilities.

For some, though, that is very difficult because it requires faith.

I work for an organization called Youth for Christ. We are committed to helping young people explore faith and discover God. I remember many years ago trying to teach this concept in a school lesson. I called out a pupil and asked him to place his trust in me by spreading out his arms and falling backwards where I would catch him. On this day, he trusted me and fell into my arms. Then I blindfolded him, asked him to trust me again and fall backwards. He did. I then spun him around, asked if he would trust me one more time and fall backwards. He did! The illustration was going to plan. I then stood in front of him, told him on the count of three if he trusted me

then he should fall backwards and I would run under his arms and catch him. Nobody ever did that – well, not until this day. What he did not know was that I had a catcher sitting nearby ready to jump up and grab him, since it would be impossible for me to run round behind him and catch him.

The young pupil started to fall backwards, but my catcher was looking out of the window (since no one had ever fallen backwards at this point). I shouted, rushed forward and tried to grab the pupil, but as I did so gravity took over and I also started to fall. The catcher jumped out of his seat. Realizing he could not catch the falling student, he lunged forwards and lifted his knee to break the young man's fall, but instead he kneed the pupil in the back of the head, which then caused me to head butt the boy as I plummeted forwards and landed on top of him as he hit the floor. The student started crying and left the class in pain. It wasn't easy to go on and teach about trust and faith after the class had watched a student put their trust in the leader and then be dropped in a shocking manner.

God says in the Bible, 'I will not let you fall.' He also says, 'I will never leave you nor let you down' (Ps. 121.3; Heb. 13.5, my version). When we allow God to be the foundation on which our lives are built, no matter what comes our way, he has our back!

For God to be the foundation of our lives requires faith. The Bible describes faith as being 'sure of the things we hope for' and 'certain of the things we cannot see' (Heb. 11.1, GNB). It is to have confidence that when we can neither hear, see nor feel something, God will still take care of us.

If you recognize that you have not allowed God to lay down new floorboards in your life, then perhaps you might want to consider doing that right now. All you need to do is to declare that you trust him, and that you are prepared to give God full control of your life. From now on, you will build everything on him rather than your own less-than-stable foundations.

When difficulties come, we are declaring hope. When things seem dark, we are believing that light will shine. When our thoughts are negative, we are seeking his positivity. When things seem uncertain, we are placing our confidence in him, and when we may want to do things a certain way that never really works, we are believing in a better way – his way.

REFLECT:

WHAT IS YOUR KEY MOTIVATOR IN LIFE? EXCELLENCE, RELATIONSHIPS, SURVIVAL, PLEASING GOD, OTHER?

WHERE DOES YOUR CONFIDENCE COME FROM – IS IT IN YOURSELF AND YOUR OWN ABILITIES, SOMEONE ELSE, OR A TRUST IN GOD? (IN TIMES OF DIFFICULTIES, DO YOU SEEK TO FIX THE PROBLEM FIRST OR PRAY FIRST?)

WHAT HAS THE GREATEST INFLUENCE OVER YOUR THOUGHTS? FRIENDS AND MEDIA OR YOUR FAITH?

MEDITATE:

YOUR WORD IS A **LAMP** TO MY FEET AND A LIGHT **TO MY PATH.**

(PS. 119.105, NASB)

ACT:

TODAY, CONSIDER MAKING A DECISION THAT YOU WILL SPEND TIME EACH DAY PRAYING AND READING PART OF THE BIBLE. A SIMPLE WAY TO PRAY IS AS FOLLOWS:

'THANK YOU, GOD' – LIST ALL THE THINGS YOU ARE THANKFUL FOR.

'SORRY, GOD' – FOR WHATEVER YOU HAVE DONE WRONG.

'PLEASE, GOD' – ASK HIM TO HELP YOU OR OTHERS WITH PARTICULAR ISSUES.

I WOULD SUGGEST THAT YOU COMMIT TO READING THE BIBLE BY READING ONE PSALM AND ONE CHAPTER OF THE NEW TESTAMENT (STARTING WITH MARK) EACH DAY.

3 WINDOWS

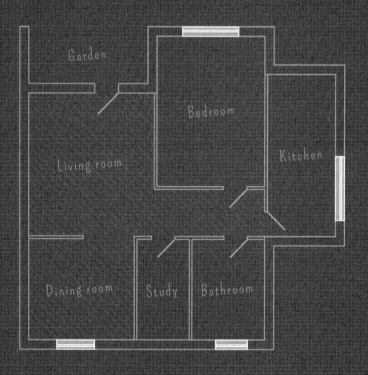

Garden

Bedroom

Kitchen

Living room

Dining room   Study   Bathroom

I love light. I am energized by the sun, and a blue sky will always have an impact on my mood for the better. How about you? I once stayed with a friend for four weeks, and he did not like sunlight. Every curtain in every room was closed and he would get upset if we opened them. After a while I started to get depressed by the lack of natural light and not being able to see the outside world. I quickly adopted the practice of leaving early in the morning and not returning until it was dark. I needed daylight!

Light not only has an impact on a person's mood but it also reveals everything around him or her.

Just a few months after I became a Christian (someone who believes in and follows Jesus), I visited one of my friends from church. We were hanging around in his bedroom chatting. I didn't really know any Christian songs at that point, but I had one line of a song stuck in my head and I just kept singing it over and over to myself. I had no idea that my singing was irritating my friend. The song was 'Look around you' with the line 'Kyrie eleison'. The Greek words mean 'Lord have mercy'. However, it wasn't the Greek words my friend was having trouble with, nor was it my singing (on this occasion). It was the words 'Look around you, can you see?' My friend suspected God was telling me to look around his bedroom because there was something to see. After a few more lines of me singing, but not knowing how he was feeling, he cracked.

'Okay, okay, I know you know!' he spluttered. I looked at him, puzzled.

'What do you mean?' I asked.

He then pulled out from under his bed a pile of pornographic magazines. He was convinced God was prompting me to look around the room because he had something to hide. He was also pretty sure I had caught a glimpse of the magazines. My friend was living with guilt.

He was really embarrassed and explained that the magazines obviously stimulated him but they also left him feeling dirty and miserable after looking at them.

Every house should have windows.

Windows not only allow the person to look out into the world but they also allow light to come into the house. Light reveals anything that has previously been hiding in the darkness. My friend had hidden something and he didn't want anyone else to see. In a sense, he wanted the curtains closed to block out the light so that a pile of porno magazines wouldn't be noticed.

If your life represents a house, do you have windows in every room? Are the curtains open and is the glass intact, or are they covered up? In other words, do you have secrets that are hidden from plain view? Are there things in your life that you would never tell another person? Things that may have happened to you or things that you have done, but either way you are doing your absolute best to keep whatever it might be in the darkness?

It makes sense to try and keep certain things covered up, away from exposure. Why revisit the past? The problem is that the past can very easily have a hold on you. Previous events can have an impact on how you feel, how you respond, decisions that you will make or avoid making, and they can fuel your dreams, giving you endless nightmares. It may seem that you have done everything to turn the light off on whatever it is that troubles you, but the reality is that most events or decisions that have troubled us turn into shadows that can often follow us wherever we go. Some shadows are always there; other shadows seem to come and go – just when it feels as though we have forgotten or finally moved on, they reappear.

I met Lauren when she was 19 years old. She was heading out on the mission field with Youth for Christ. She shared a story that has stuck with me. It was a story that resulted in freedom.

When Lauren was 16, she had a boyfriend; he had come over to her house and, just before he was leaving, they started to kiss. After a while, Lauren pulled away and said she needed to get her homework done, but her boyfriend was clearly turned on and wanted more. Lauren didn't want more, but nevertheless ended up sleeping with him. She didn't enjoy it; she didn't want to sleep with him, and the entire time she was more concerned that her parents would walk in and so wanted it over as quickly as possible. Until that moment, Lauren had been a virgin and had no wish for her first experience to be like that.

Upon reflection, Lauren believed she had been violated. She didn't resist, so the word violation seemed strong, but that's how she felt. She allowed her boyfriend to undress her, she didn't resist and she didn't scream. While she didn't tell him to stop, she felt she had implied that she didn't want to do it. She never told anyone about what had happened to her. To make matters worse, the next day her boyfriend dumped her. Eventually she was able to shrug off the event and tried to move on. That attempt, however, was short-lived. A few months later, Lauren discovered that she was pregnant.

HAVE YOU EVER BEEN IN A
SITUATION
WHERE THERE WERE
NO GOOD OPTIONS?

WHAT HELPED YOU TO MAKE YOUR
DECISION?

At 16 years of age you don't have many choices, and none of them may seem good. You can have the baby, but then you have to look after that tiny little life and it will severely impact your education and social life, or you can have the baby adopted, but that means someone else is raising your child. Your third option is to have an abortion and terminate the life within.

Lauren's parents were Christians, and while Lauren went to church she wasn't really sure where she was at with her faith, but she did believe that an abortion was ending the life of an unborn baby and that God would not want that to happen.

Just like countless other girls in a similar situation to Lauren, she tried to do everything she could to miscarry. Weeks went by and, no matter how hard she tried, that baby was growing and forming inside her and she was putting on weight. She was getting desperate and after receiving professional counsel she decided to have an abortion.

An appointment was made, Lauren turned up and had the surgery. Afterwards she got down from the table and the nurse pushed her away in a wheelchair. At that moment the reality of what she had just done hit her and she began to cry. The nurse bent over and whispered in her ear, 'If you don't stop crying, I will take you back in there and we will scrape you out all over again!' Lauren had never felt more lonely.

As the months went by, the trauma and guilt of having an abortion began to eat into her. She tried to move on, but was struggling to do so. Her school grades plummeted, she lost a considerable amount of weight and she no longer went out with her friends. Lauren was miserable. She hadn't told a single person about what had happened to her.

So what happened next came as a complete shock. One day, as she walked through the kitchen, her mum blocked her path, looked her in the eye and said, 'Lauren, have you had an abortion?' The question came out of nowhere and it was specific. She didn't ask her whether she was in trouble or whether something had happened, but whether she had had an abortion. For the very first time Lauren was confronted with the truth. She could neither confirm nor deny it, but her body took over. She began to shake, and the floodgates opened; Lauren started to sob. Her mum led her to the rocking chair, placed her 16-year-old daughter on her knee and held her so tight, saying over and over again, 'Lauren, I am so sorry and I love you so much!'

She had not expected that reaction from her parents; she had expected to be judged, condemned and rejected for taking the life of an unborn baby. Instead, she received love, grace and acceptance.

The light cancelled out the darkness and exposed a 16-year-old's traumatic journey that had until that point changed her life for the worse. Now the truth was out, and she was suddenly free, accepted and loved. The 19-year-old Lauren that I met had been transformed and was a very happy young woman.

I recently told that same story at a youth event in London. At the end I invited anyone who would like to become a follower of Jesus to come to the front where we would pray for them. An 18-year-old girl came down to the front and spoke to one of the leaders. This girl was not your average 18-year-old. She was the leader of a fairly formidable local gang. They had stood on the street corner and watched a stream of young people go into the building. Out of curiosity they followed, and the entire gang walked into the church hall that night. The youth leader asked why she had responded to the message,

THE LORD IS

CLOSE

TO THE

BROKEN-
HEARTED.

(PS. 34.18, NIV)

and she replied, 'That man was telling my story.' The youth leader was confused. 'What story?' The girl explained that only last week she had had an abortion and she had not told anyone, even her mum. She concluded by saying, 'But I feel so dirty.'

Lauren had had something traumatic happen to her that resulted in an abortion. The gang leader had slept around and willingly chosen to have an abortion. Both had been left feeling uncomfortable by the experience. Whether we have done something or had something done to us, if it has resulted in our feeling guilty or bad, our natural tendency is to hide whatever it might be, close the curtain and pretend it never happened. In the short term that strategy might work; longer term it will most likely haunt us. So what stops us from opening the curtain and bringing the issue to light?

Shame.

Shame will cripple us.

There is a story in the Bible about a woman who had done something terrible by the standards of the times in which she lived. She had committed adultery. Her sentence was death. The authorities wanted to know what Jesus would do, so they dragged the woman before Jesus in all her shame. Jesus saw past her guilt and her crime to her worth. He was moved by compassion and set her free. Not only was she pardoned from a death sentence but she was also forgiven for what she had done before God. She was truly free.

It is really important to understand in the context of this chapter that it isn't about whether a person has had an affair outside marriage, or an abortion; it isn't about the punishment, or even the judgement, or the ethics of whether it was right or wrong, but rather what impact the experience has had on a person. Trauma, difficult life choices, or decisions we might wish we could change, can leave us with scars. It is the impact of the scars that I think, right now, Jesus is most interested in addressing.

Jesus has already seen what is hidden under the bed. He has seen the nightmares that you relive, and he has seen what you have done and what has been done to you. He asks only one thing: that you allow him to open the curtains, let light shine on the darkness and reveal what you are trying to hide from him.

Consider, today, allowing the windows to be opened on your life. Don't hold back on what God would like to do in your life. He wants to bring healing, forgiveness and health. He can only do that if we are willing to admit there are things we are hiding from him. We need to be brave. We need to be strong enough to open the curtains and allow Jesus to walk into a well-lit room that has things inside that may bring shame or pain. He does not seek to condemn us; he seeks to bring us life-changing freedom.

REFLECT:

ARE THERE THINGS IN YOUR LIFE THAT
YOU ARE HIDING FROM OTHER PEOPLE?
PERHAPS HABITS OR PAST EVENTS?

DO THOSE THINGS BRING PAIN OR
SHAME OR BOTH?

ARE YOU WILLING TO ALLOW JESUS TO
SEE THE THINGS IN YOUR LIFE THAT YOU
HAVE HIDDEN FROM OTHERS?

MEDITATE:

THERE IS NOW
NO
CONDEMNATION
FOR THOSE WHO ARE IN
**CHRIST
JESUS.**

(ROM. 8.1, NIV)

ACT:

PRAY THIS PRAYER IF YOU ARE ABLE:

**JESUS, THERE ARE THINGS THAT HAVE
HAPPENED IN MY LIFE. THEY ARE_____
_____
_____
_____
AND I NEED YOU EITHER TO FORGIVE ME
WHERE I HAVE DONE WRONG OR TO REMIND
ME THAT I AM STILL OF WORTH AND VALUE
AND THAT WHAT HAS HAPPENED TO ME
DOES NOT MAKE ME A LESSER PERSON.
PLEASE HELP ME TO DEAL WITH SHAME;
HELP ME TO BE HEALED; AND REMIND ME
OF HOW MUCH YOU LOVE AND ACCEPT ME.
HELP ME NOW TO LIVE IN FREEDOM.**

MY EXPERIENCE TELLS ME THAT, AS JESUS BEGINS TO BRING LIGHT ON
THINGS THAT HAVE BEEN HIDDEN, WE CAN REMEMBER EVENTS IN MORE
DETAIL AND FEEL VULNERABLE. I SUGGEST THAT, IF YOU HAVE HAD
SOMETHING TRAUMATIC HAPPEN TO YOU, YOU ARE BRAVE ENOUGH TO
TELL SOMEONE WITH WHOM YOU FEEL SAFE AND WHO CAN HELP YOU
TO RECOVER FULLY. I BELIEVE JESUS CAN AND WILL BRING FREEDOM,
BUT HE OFTEN USES OTHERS IN THAT PROCESS.

4 WALLS

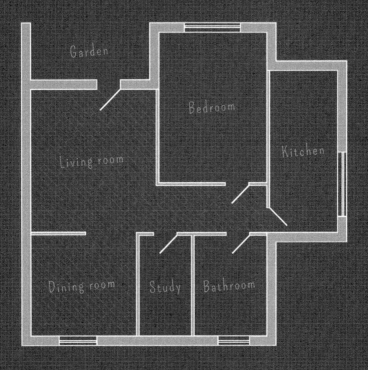

Garden

Bedroom

Kitchen

Living room

Dining room

Study

Bathroom

My wife is called Joy, and she loves colours. Bright colours, to be specific. Houses are beautiful or ugly to my wife based on their colour. They can be elegant and structurally sound mansions but they are of far less value in her eyes if they are dull in colour (even though such houses may be hugely expensive!). Colour matters, so therefore image matters.

I have met a number of people (both male and female) who have suffered with anorexia. Most would starve themselves of food, and when they did eat more than the tiny portions they would normally allow themselves, quite often they would force themselves to vomit shortly afterwards. To me they looked like skin and bone, but when they looked in the mirror they viewed themselves as fat. Somewhere along the way they had bought into the narrative that in order to be attractive they needed to be considerably underweight. I recognize I am oversimplifying anorexia and for some it is not necessarily about appearance, but for others it is.

I have met women and girls who will not leave the house until they have spent hours putting on their make-up. They won't answer the door or dare step outside until they feel they look stunning. Not to wear make-up is to be naked. This is how their beauty is defined.

I have met guys who spend hours working out in the gym, obsessed with the need to put in an hour before and after work. Their body is a temple and they need to have a well-defined six-pack. Their physique defines them.

WHAT HAPPENS WHEN YOU
PANIC?

I have walked into many a room where people have stopped whatever it was they were doing and lowered their eyes to my shoes and slowly moved their gaze upwards scanning my jeans and shirt, finishing with my hair. I am not very image-conscious. I am more than okay if I don't shave every day, and I cut my hair roughly every six weeks. If that's not bad enough, I am not well groomed either. My eyebrows, if left too long, look like hedgehogs pinned to my forehead, and there are probably a few baby chicks hiding in my ears. But I recognize that for other people image is a statement. To look sharp and well groomed is a big deal.

Image does matter to me, but in different ways.

A few years ago I got up to speak at a church and, just as I was about to share, I started to have a panic attack. Since the day I became a Christian, my life had been free from any real anxiety, but 20 years later it came back with a vengeance. If you have never had a panic attack then it might seem a strange concept. For me, a panic attack starts with an internal sense of hollowness, and the bottom falls out of my confidence, which then usually results in my voice sounding very nervous, quickly followed by a sense of not being able to breathe or at least regulate my breathing, so I start to gasp for air; my throat tightens and my chest hurts. Finally, I start to shake. So that day I looked and sounded an absolute mess. The audience also started to feel nervous and tense because they could see that I was not handling the moment very well. I got through it. Realizing I couldn't deceive anyone, I made light of my reaction, and my confidence suddenly returned. I have had a number of panic attacks since then. They have never been pleasant and I am always left feeling exhausted.

When Jesus knocked on the door of my life at 16 years old and I let him in, the major issues I was struggling with as a teenager were resolved as he brought hope, love and forgiveness. But as the architect continued to move from room to room, inspecting the cracks and examining the woodwork, 20 years later he touched on something that was hidden from plain view and he began to address the dry rot in the walls. My problem came down to image. It had nothing to do with my weight, my fitness or how well groomed I might appear, but rather how I viewed and felt about myself.

The outside of our house has bright yellow walls, which obviously pleases my wife. However, it wasn't until we had lived in our home for a few months that we realized there was a sizeable crack in the outside wall that went from the ground all the way up to the roof. It wasn't obvious at a glance and the vast majority of people never noticed it, but once I had seen it, I couldn't help but notice it.

More often than not, many of the issues that we battle with in our lives are not obvious to other people, but they are more than obvious to ourselves. Those issues will then define how we feel, which results in how we act and behave.

The old saying of 'sticks and stones may break my bones but words will never harm me' is simply not true. Children who are told that they are not very bright or not very good at sports often go on to be haunted by those comments. I broke my foot as a teenager. It hurt then and in cold weather it can still hurt now, years later, even though the bone has healed. When we are told something hurtful we feel it deeply at the time, but we can also still feel it years later. We don't have to break something to feel significant pain. The average girl is made

WHAT TRIGGERS PANIC FOR YOU?

aware around the age of five that beauty is about how pretty she looks. Only when she fails to meet the exceptional standards of what defines beauty do people start to switch to a new tag line and tell her that beauty is actually about character, saying that 'real beauty is on the inside'. As a boy I was told that to be a man I needed to be tough and rough. To be honest, I am neither. So, am I a man? Biologically, yes, there can be no dispute! But by the standards of the world, who knows?

How we see ourselves is often through the lenses of other people, and there lies a very big problem. Most people's standards are unattainable – much of society will tell you that you are never going to be good enough. To be blond is to be a bimbo; to be bright is to be a nerd; to be a nerd is to be a social misfit; to have personality is to be ugly; to be athletic is to be dumb; and on and on go the grossly distorted generalizations. Who are we trying to please?

When I had my first panic attack in public, as I was heading to the stage, my brain started to have a rather loud conversation with me: 'Everyone in this room is brighter than you and far more gifted than you are; most people communicate to bigger audiences. You are not good enough!' By the time I reached the stage I was a wreck.

Dr Deepak Chopra believes our brain has between 60,000 and 80,000 thoughts a day. The vast majority are subconscious, and, of these, 80 per cent are negative. The brain throughout the day is whispering phrases such as: 'What if . . .'; 'You can't . . .'; 'They won't . . .'; 'That will never . . .'

Those few words can have a devastating snowball effect. Let me explain: my car ride to work is roughly 20 minutes. On one particular day, as I got into the car in a fairly good mood, I had a 'What if . . .' thought, which was quickly followed by further negative phrases. I didn't break my cycle of thinking, and when I got out of the car at the office I was feeling incredibly low and mad with pretty much every member of my team at the office (who had done nothing wrong). I had allowed my mind to paint a very negative view of my world. I went from one negative thought to another.

Whether you have dry rot or cracks in your walls, it needs dealing with because your walls determine how you view your house, or more specifically, how you feel about yourself.

My wife and I have four children. When they were much younger all they cared about was how Mummy and Daddy felt about them. Recent research also confirms that teenagers ultimately want to make their parents proud of them. How their parents view them matters. Somewhere along the way we start wanting others to like us and to be impressed by us, and that has an impact on our behaviour and even our values. It's more than okay to want people to like us, but when that starts to define who we are and how we behave, we have started to listen to a narrative that says we only matter if people like us or are proud of us. So, if we think they do not, or we act inappropriately to gain their approval, we are in trouble.

When Jesus started to expose the dry rot in my life, I realized that what other people thought about me mattered hugely, to the point that I no longer believed I had any real value unless people were impressed by me. The real defining moment came when I had to answer the following question: 'Do I care more about what the world thinks, with its unobtainable inconsistent standards, or do I care

READ PSALM 139.13–17

CIRCLE
WHAT YOU LIKE.

QUESTION
WHAT YOU ARE NOT SURE OF.

UNDERLINE
WHAT YOU NEED HELP TO BELIEVE.

more about what God thinks, who made me, loves me and set the universe into being?'

As Jesus looks at the walls in your life, he doesn't look at them the same way that you or others might. He looks at you and says, 'You are amazing. Sure, there are a few things we need to work on, but you are incredible.' The reason he says that is because he put you here on planet earth and you belong to him. What he actually says is this:

What can stop me from loving you? Can trouble or difficulties or bullying or poverty or nakedness or danger or weapons or destruction? . . . Neither death nor life, neither angels nor demons, neither the present nor the future, nor any powers, neither height nor depth, nor anything else in all creation, will be able to separate you from my love!
(Rom. 8.35–39, my version)

You have a choice, as do I: we can either listen to our own inner voice telling us that for whatever reason we will never truly live up to the expectations of this world, or we can listen to the Architect who made us and says, 'You are amazing and nothing can stop me from thinking that, or from loving you.'

In Psalm 139 David (the author) reflects on God and how God created and sees us:

You made all the delicate, inner parts of
    my body
   and knit me together in my mother's
     womb.
Thank you for making me so
    wonderfully complex!
   Your workmanship is marvellous –
    and how well I know it.
You watched me as I was being formed
    in utter seclusion,
   as I was woven together in the dark
    of the womb.
You saw me before I was born.
   Every day of my life was recorded in
    your book.
Every moment was laid out
   before a single day had passed.

How precious are your thoughts about
    me, O God!
   They are innumerable!
I can't even count them;
   they outnumber the grains of sand!
(Ps. 139.13–17, NLT)

I am not sure how that makes you feel, but the fact that God thinks about me more times than there are grains of sand, and that he designed me and considers me wonderful, is both incredible and humbling. Why then do we so often see ourselves very differently from how God sees us? How is it that we struggle to value ourselves when the Creator of all life loves us so deeply? We need to ask God to allow us to feel his love and his value for us, and to deal with any dry rot that may have taken hold deep within the walls of our lives.

REFLECT:

WHO ARE YOU MOST TRYING TO PLEASE BY THE WAY YOU BEHAVE OR APPEAR?

IF OTHERS DON'T COMPLIMENT YOU ON HOW YOU LOOK OR PERFORM, HOW DOES THAT MAKE YOU FEEL? WHY?

WHAT WOULD IT TAKE TO LIVE IN SUCH A WAY THAT ALL YOU REALLY WANT TO DO IS PLEASE GOD RATHER THAN PLEASE ANYONE ELSE?

MEDITATE:

DON'T COPY THE BEHAVIOUR AND CUSTOMS OF THIS WORLD, BUT **LET GOD TRANSFORM YOU** INTO A NEW PERSON BY **CHANGING** THE WAY YOU THINK.

(ROM. 12.2, NLT)

ACT:

IT HAS BEEN SCIENTIFICALLY PROVED THAT POSITIVE THOUGHTS CREATE POSITIVE FEELINGS. IT HAS ALSO BEEN PROVED THAT REPETITIVE ACTION CREATES LONG-TERM HABITS…SO WHY NOT, EVERY TIME YOU FEEL LOW OR UPSET OR HAVE NEGATIVE THOUGHTS, COMMIT TO SAYING THE FOLLOWING, OVER AND OVER?

GIVE THANKS TO THE LORD, FOR HE IS GOOD, HIS LOVE ENDURES FOR EVER. (PS. 136.1, NIV)

FOCUS ON ONE DIFFERENT WORD EACH TIME YOU SAY THE FULL VERSE AND EMPHASIZE THAT WORD, STARTING WITH 'GIVE'. IN ORDER TO DO THAT, YOU WILL NEED TO SAY IT 13 TIMES. REWIRE YOUR BRAIN BY REMINDING YOURSELF HOW MUCH GOD LOVES YOU!

5 ROOF

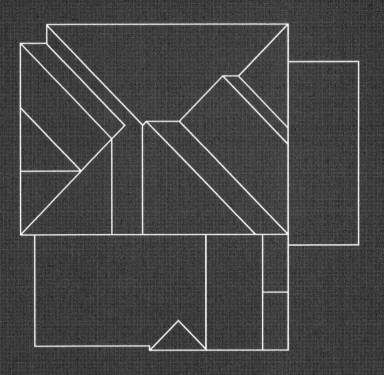

'Stop going to church!'

'No!' replied the 16-year-old boy who had just informed his Muslim parents that he had become a Christian. They locked him in his bedroom and told him he could not come out until he had given up on his new faith. He responded, 'As soon as you open the door I will go to church!' That was possibly not the right way to win over concerned parents, but he was passionate about his new faith and didn't think anyone had the right to tell him what he could or could not believe.

After a few weeks, his parents recognized that their son was not going to change his mind, so they stopped feeding him in the hope that his appetite would help him come around to their way of thinking. Instead, the boy lost weight and his health began to decline.

In despair, this Middle Eastern family informed the religious police hoping they could help. What happened next nobody had anticipated. The police walked into the house, grabbed the boy's hand, took out a knife and sliced off a finger nail. They then sliced off a second. When they were about to remove a third, the boy screamed out, 'Okay, okay, I will stop going to church!' The police cleaned their knife, threw a bandage at the boy and walked out of the house.

That 16-year-old later told me, 'They can stop me from going to church, but they cannot stop me from believing in Jesus Christ!'

There is much about that story that is shocking. In the West we do not face torture or imprisonment for our beliefs. The likelihood is that you will never face any external problems as a result of being

HOW DOES THIS VERSE MAKE YOU FEEL?

TERRIFIED
EXCITED
POSITIVE
NOTHING
CONCERN
OTHER · OKAY · WORRIED

a Christian. You may be teased or people may not agree with you, but it won't result in torture.

Storms in life, however, are never far away. Jesus' brother James wrote to the very first Christians to tell them to expect difficulties and that when they did face them they should not be discouraged but see it as an opportunity to let their character be refined. Being a Christian does not mean your life will be free from problems: you will have your fair share. However, God promises to be with you in those storms. How you respond in difficult times is what matters the most.

Recently I had roofers come and inspect the roof of my house. Before they even got on a ladder they said that the guttering needed fixing and something about the chimney needing to be rendered. To be honest, I switched off as the foreman explained, because I'm not a roofer and I just wanted my roof to be in good order. He quoted me an amount to fix it and we agreed a date that he would come. A few days later, I was at work when I received an urgent call from the roofer. He said that once he got on to my roof he noticed that the tarred felt on our kitchen extension was worn and whoever had laid it had only put down a temporary surface rather than a permanent one. He sent me pictures that showed worrying holes, and even one of a large bush growing out of the roof. It needed to be fixed and it needed to be fixed now. However, the bill was massive! What choice did I have? There was evidence of water already getting through. Nobody wants a leak, because the roof protects the entire house from rain, storms and the cold.

If there is a hole in a roof, then over time water will penetrate, damaging other areas of the house. The hole will also create a draught and fail to keep the house warm and safe. A hole matters.

If your life represents a house, is your roof sealed? Let me ask a different question. When storms hit, do you panic, react unwisely and begin to doubt? It is natural to do that. However, God promises to watch over us and to be with us. The storm may be all around us, but is water pouring in? Do we look for Jesus in the storm?

Jesus found himself in a dramatic storm while on a lake. It was so bad that his disciples (followers), many of whom were experienced fishermen, were convinced they were going to die. The waves were high, and the water must have been crashing inside the boat. The disciples were so terrified that they looked for Jesus, only to find him sleeping. They woke Jesus up and asked how he could be sleeping at a time like this, when they were surely all about to die. There was nothing about the storm that disturbed Jesus. It had not caught him by surprise and he wasn't worried about the outcome. He had peace, unlike his disciples. Jesus stood up and commanded the storm to stop, and the chaos immediately ended. The waters were calm and peace returned.

There may be times when it feels as if Jesus is fast asleep when storms hit our lives, causing us to panic and leaving us crippled by fear, but it is important to recognize that Jesus has not been caught by surprise. He knows what is going on and he is not distant; he is with you. It may feel as if he is asleep, but the reality is that Jesus is not panicking. He has peace. A leaking roof comes when we allow the storms to overwhelm us. We quickly turn our eyes from Jesus to the raging issues! Obviously we should not ignore the problems, but we need to take comfort in the reality that Jesus is in the boat with us. The boat is not going to sink. Things may not go the way we want: the fence may blow down and a tree may be uprooted leaving a mess in the garden, but the house is still standing.

When we moved back from the USA to the UK, our son stayed in the USA to study, but our three girls moved with us. None of them had ever lived in the UK. Even though they were British passport holders who had visited their grandparents over numerous summer holidays, the UK had never really been home. So when they started in school they had a few cultural adjustments to make.

My middle daughter, whom I will call 'M', entered year 8. At first she was of interest to her classmates – she had a different accent, had been born overseas and had lived in three other nations.

It wasn't long, though, before she was being made fun of for being different. The teasing turned to something more serious. One day she came home with a swollen face, where someone had hit her. As parents we registered our complaints and the school promised to keep her safe, but they couldn't make the other students like M. At break times my daughter would usually spend all of her time sitting in the toilet cubicles because it was the only place people could not find her to mock her. However, even the cubicles turned out to be unsafe, because all over the walls were written horrible comments about her. M was lonely and hurting. One day she left her school bag on the other side of the cubicle and someone who had recognized M's bag deliberately forced themselves to vomit into it. The content of someone's stomach was now all over her school books. We were increasingly worried for our daughter. She had always been full of life and energy; now she was quiet and disinterested. Her roof almost certainly had a leak, but she wasn't talking about it. Something had to change.

In a religious education class that M attended at school, her teacher referred to Jesus as an idiot. In her opinion, Jesus was an animal abuser for riding a donkey! M, despite all her challenges, held on to her faith and objected to the teacher's remarks. She received a harsh rebuke for challenging the teacher. As parents we felt enough was enough. We had talked to the school about the bullying and now a teacher had given our daughter a hard time for her faith. We took our daughter out of the school and moved her to one further away from where we lived. It was a game changer. M quickly made friends and started to thrive. It was a drastic move and one that we didn't enter into lightly, but she is now the girl that we remember rather than the shell she had become.

Bullying can be devastating. Sometimes the issues can be resolved quickly, other times they linger. However, Jesus promises to be with you in the storm, whether it be bullying, an illness, or your parents losing their jobs and becoming unemployed. Nothing surprises Jesus! There is peace available. He asks us to draw close to him in the storms and he will draw close to us. He promises to work to the good in the difficulties, and he will stay with us. He is to be trusted, and relied upon. He is with us.

All storms eventually end. We can either panic and run around like headless chickens or we can tell God we are frightened and need his help, and ask that he will give us peace and comfort.

When storms hit my life, I panic, I really do. I can't pretend otherwise. But I quickly recognize that I am panicking and shift my focus

HE GOT UP, REBUKED THE WIND AND SAID TO THE WAVES, 'QUIET! BE STILL!' THEN THE WIND DIED DOWN AND IT WAS COMPLETELY CALM.

(MARK 4.39, NIV)

from the storm to Jesus, who I know can command the storm to be silent. But until he does, I need his peace to endure whatever is happening around me. How do I know that he will provide peace and ultimately silence the storm? Because the Bible tells me that he will; it is a promise. What's more, experience confirms it. I have watched God end the storms almost immediately, and I have had storms rage for years on end; regardless of how long they last, he is always with us. He calls us to be still (don't rush into panic mode) and know that he is God (able, in control and with you).

For five years we lived in Thailand, where it is green and lush. We had come from the barren deserts of the Middle East, so the contrast was spectacular. We actually lived in Chiang Mai, which is surrounded by mountains, with beautiful dense forestry. The presence of the mountains never failed to impress. They were close and they were bold. However, for three months of the year, the farmers burned the fields, and the atmosphere was so polluted that there was a constant haze over the city. In that time the mountains would completely disappear. After four weeks you would forget that the city is surrounded by mountains, and after eight weeks you would wonder if they were really there at all. Then came the rainy season and the pollution would quickly lift, and the visible presence of the mountains returned. The mountains had always been there; we just couldn't see them. So often it feels as if God might not be there. He calls us to trust him whether we see, hear or feel his presence or not. He asks that we believe he is with us. Finding peace in the storm is choosing to believe that God is with us even if we can see no evidence of him. As we draw close he provides reminders along the way that he is with us until the storm stills and the pollution lifts to reveal his presence.

When the storms hit your metaphorical house (your life), does the roof leak and cause further damage by the manner in which you panic, react and stress, or is your roof watertight because you find yourself able to draw close to God, whether you sense him or not, and find his peace? A 16-year-old boy endured torture and faced a huge 'storm', but that did not deter him from believing God and seeking him. My daughter was bullied, but it didn't stop her from pushing forward in her faith in the midst of the storm. I have endured numerous storms and have been able to find his peace until the raging conditions end. I don't always get it right, I sometimes panic even when I have pushed into his presence, but I simply have to refocus and recognize that the only way through is by trusting God and seeking his peace.

There will be times when the challenges are too big for us to cope on our own, and we need others to step in and help. Bullying is a good example of when we should not keep quiet, but rather need to tell others what is happening. While telling others, we should also be telling Jesus and drawing close to him.

Are there holes in your roof that you need to ask Jesus to help you address? Then the next time the storms come (because there will always be a next time) you can rest even as chaos surrounds you, and trust that he will see you through.

REFLECT:

HOW DO I REACT WHEN PROBLEMS PRESENT THEMSELVES? DO I GET STRESSED AND ANXIOUS AND TRY TO FIX THEM, OFTEN MAKING THE SITUATION WORSE? DO I HIDE AND BURY MY HEAD PRETENDING NOTHING IS HAPPENING? AM I CALM AND RATIONAL AND THINK THROUGH ALL THE OPTIONS BEFORE ACTING? OR DO I FOCUS ON JESUS, SEEK HIS PEACE AND ASK FOR HIS HELP BEFORE I DO ANYTHING ELSE?

MEDITATE:

DON'T WORRY ABOUT ANYTHING; INSTEAD, **PRAY** ABOUT EVERYTHING. TELL GOD WHAT YOU NEED, AND **THANK HIM** FOR ALL HE HAS DONE.

(PHIL. 4.6, NLT)

ACT:

THE AUTHOR PAUL IN THE BIBLE TELLS US TO PRAY, TELL GOD WHAT WE NEED AND THANK HIM FOR WHAT HE HAS DONE IN THE PAST. PAUL ASKS US TO THANK GOD FOR WHAT HE HAS DONE BECAUSE IT QUICKLY REMINDS US OF HIS FAITHFULNESS IN THE PAST, HOW HE WAS WITH US IN THE STORMS AND WHAT HAPPENED, AND IT BUILDS WITHIN US A GRATEFUL HEART.

LET ME ENCOURAGE YOU TO DO TWO THINGS...

1 START A JOURNAL TODAY – BUY A BLANK BOOK AND RECORD ALL THE WAYS IN WHICH GOD ANSWERS PRAYERS, OR HOW HE WORKS IN YOUR LIFE. DO THIS ON A DAILY/WEEKLY BASIS.

2 IN TIMES OF DIFFICULTIES, READ AND REREAD WHAT GOD HAS DONE! LET IT BOOST YOUR FAITH AND CONFIDENCE. TAKE TIME TO THANK HIM FOR HIS PAST FAITHFULNESS IN THE CERTAINTY THAT SOMEHOW HE WILL HELP YOU IN YOUR CURRENT STORMS.

6 LIVING ROOM

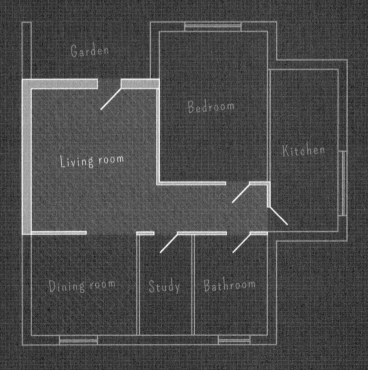

Garden

Bedroom

Kitchen

Living room

Dining room   Study   Bathroom

I am fairly messy, and in certain areas of my life I am seriously disorganized!

Because of that, there is nothing that frustrates me more than someone turning up at my house unannounced. The unexpected sound of a doorbell will take me from a happy place sitting watching TV, surrounded by mugs, plates and various clothes (shoes, socks, my discarded coat), to instant stress and grumpiness. My living room is not fit for visitors. I don't want people walking into my private space in such a state of chaos. I need warning so that I can tidy up and then pretend that my living room is always clean and tidy.

When Jesus walks into the living room of your life, you might momentarily feel concerned by its general messiness. However, it won't be the odd sock stuffed behind a cushion, the dirty plate with mould under the chair, or the crisp packet sitting idly next to the bin that catches his attention. Nor will it be the mismatch in colours between the carpet, wallpaper and curtains. Jesus is far more interested in what happens in this room, and how you spend your time here, than whether it is neat and colour-coordinated.

For most people, the living room is where they relax and recharge. It's where the main TV and Wi-Fi router are usually located, and it is also where the comfy seats are. It is a safe place to veg, slob and be you! This room is important. It is where you live, and it's where you can escape from the world. Often others share this space with you, people you know and trust.

It is the place to rest and relax.

HOW DO YOU SPEND YOUR

TIME?

LIST YOUR TOP FIVE:

1

2

3

4

5

To rest and relax is so important that God commands us to do it. That's right – he says we must do it! (Check out Exodus 23.12.) He knows that we get tired and stressed with life and that we need not only sleep but down time. So there are two questions that I am guessing will be of great interest to Jesus:

1 How do you actually rest and relax?
2 How often do you rest and relax?

The way I switch off is probably very different from the way you might.

Give me a burger and endless hours of watching the sports channel and I couldn't be happier.

I've unofficially named one of my daughters '2 per cent' because every night she switches over from the TV show that I'm watching to some senseless series that she only watches 2 per cent of the time; the remaining 98 per cent she spends on her device, communicating with people all over the world. The TV show merely creates background noise. When I get home, I don't want to talk to anyone other than my family, and they want to talk to everyone anywhere apart from me, who just so happens to be in the room with them! So why then can't I just watch my show?

At Youth for Christ, we did a piece of research to find out exactly how young people spend their spare time. The top five answers were as follows:

- Watching YouTube – 81 per cent
- Watching TV and films – 77 per cent
- Using social media – 74 per cent
- Spending time with friends – 73 per cent
- Gaming – 61 per cent

When I look at that list, three of those would have been in my top three when I was a teenager (watching TV, spending time with friends, and gaming). However, how people do those three things now has changed massively.

First, when I was a teenager the internet didn't exist! Today, 94 per cent of young people use the internet frequently; they have never known life without it and most TV shows they watch are either streamed online or downloaded. Second, when I watched TV there was one single box in the corner of the room and everyone stared at it. Most houses now have TVs that are flat, stick to the wall and are nearly the size of a bedsheet. However, when it comes to watching something, it's completely normal for each person to have their own device and watch or do whatever they like regardless of what is on the TV (like my 2 per cent daughter).

There is nothing wrong with any of these top five ways to relax! However, I suspect Jesus is interested in the detail.

What you watch

Whether it be YouTube, TV or films, would you be happy for Jesus to sit down next to you? Would you feel comfortable with him watching whatever is on your screen?

Before you answer that, let me ask you a different question: would you be okay with one of your parents, grandparents or guardians watching it with you?

I don't ask my children what they watch, but when they stop watching or shuffle nervously when I walk into the room, then I suddenly get really curious. My presence has made them feel awkward. Whatever they are watching is not Dad-appropriate. Which means it's also probably not Jesus-appropriate.

Just to be clear – I am not remotely close to being on the same level as Jesus, but they know I have standards for what we should be filling our minds with. I can almost hear you groan, because it is probably the same in your house. So, when you are on your own, do you watch things that may not pass the Mum- or Dad-appropriate list? I think people can quickly come up with good reasons, such as 'their standards are for old people, the world has changed and I just need to keep the peace when they are around, but when they are not . . .'. That makes sense.

What's wrong with people talking about sex, a really good fight scene, colourful language (which you hear every day at school), and why is nudity a problem? Seeing people having sex on TV is not the same as you having sex. Being a teenager is all about learning, isn't it? Nobody wants to learn about sex from their parents, or talk about relationships, and adults seem to be against fighting and general violence – therefore the media is a much better teacher!

All very fair points – so does that make it okay?

Paul tells us in the Bible to think about things that are good for us. That is not a bad shout. There is plenty of research that supports the idea that we act out what we see. So what we see becomes really important.

In an experiment, a group of small children watched adults act in a violent manner towards their play dolls. Those same children then started to show aggressive behaviour to other people. Some years ago there was the true and tragic case of a toddler being killed by two older children. Upon investigation, it was found that the older children had recently watched a violent movie and then copied in their behaviour towards the toddler what they had seen in the movie.

What we see leaves an imprint on our memory and can never be wiped away. Worse, if we watch something often enough, we can become desensitized (no longer moved or shocked by something that is moving or shocking) and we can start to believe something is okay, even if we previously believed it to be wrong.

When Jesus walks into the living room of your life, he sees the couch and the TV, the laptop on your knee and the smart phone in your hand. He becomes really interested in how you spend your time in this room. Jesus is not a joy stealer. He is not against what you do or watch. However, he understands the complex, sensitive and fragile nature of our minds.

When Paul in the Bible talked about renewing (renovating) and transforming our minds, he was aware that our minds dominate our actions, thoughts, beliefs and how we see the world. If we continually fill our minds with things that are opposite to how the Bible suggests we should live, then the outcome will be that we start to change our beliefs and views and ultimately our behaviour.

What then is shaping your thoughts?

YouTube, TV and films are not in themselves wrong, but their content is the issue. Consider watching things that do not contradict your beliefs but strengthen them. Then what you watch will eventually shape how you think. That is not to say you have to turn off the TV when there is a fight scene, or gasp when someone swears, but common sense needs to take the lead in decision-making. If it is an 18 or restricted movie then it is probably full of violence or sex or adult content. I don't watch 18 (or restricted) movies for that reason. I also review in advance any 15 view ratings for the same reason. The question you need to be able to answer before you watch anything is whether it will have a positive, neutral or negative impact on the values that you hold as a Christian.

If you are a guy and attracted to girls, seeing a woman's naked chest in a movie is almost certainly going to turn you on – it just is! How will such images affect how you relate to women? Will you start to perceive them as objects? If you watch enough reality shows where the main theme is about dysfunctional relationships and everyone is being horrible to each other, don't be surprised to find they shape how you talk to other people or view them.

Your mind is precious, and how you shape it will have a significant impact on how you live your life. Jesus wants to watch TV with you, so you should ask yourself, when your conscience starts to tug, whether you are comfortable with him sitting beside you watching this particular show. If not, consider turning it off or turning to another channel.

How you use social media

When I was a teenager, my dad had a mobile phone. It was the size of a brick. The battery pack alone was bigger than my face. It was revolutionary! Bulky, impractical and ugly, it was nevertheless a game changer. Someone could phone you anywhere and at any time without a wire! The phone, however, only made or took calls. Texting hadn't been thought of, the internet didn't exist, so emailing, surfing the web and social media were not even imagined.

According to our research at Youth for Christ, 82 per cent of young people use social media every day. Most have smart phones, which have the ability to access almost any information that exists. Alongside that, friends and family can communicate 24/7 free of charge (depending on your package) and in an instant by calling, texting, sending an image or through video chat that enables you to be connected to anyone anywhere. Compared to my dad's basic brick phone, the world has become unbelievably interesting very quickly.

So, here is the thing: technology is advancing at such a rate that it is changing and redefining all previous and traditional ways of communicating and learning. It is reshaping the boundaries of what we consider to be acceptable, and we haven't thought through the impact of such a revolution on how we behave and communicate.

Let me give you an example.

I have a friend who was summoned to his daughter's school, only to be told that she had taken a picture of herself naked and sent it on to her boyfriend. He in turn had sent it to his friends, and the picture of the 16-year-old had gone viral within a day. My friend was told that the police had been informed and it very quickly became an investigation that led to multiple prosecutions for sexting. His daughter was embarrassed and ashamed, and her boyfriend (along with many others) found himself in trouble with the police. He and others received criminal records.

There is nothing about that story that will surprise you. It's now common practice for people to send intimate pictures of themselves.

Social media in itself is not wrong or bad; it can be incredibly positive and powerful. We just haven't thought through how to control its power.

Anxiety, depression, self-harm and attempted suicide have all increased among young people, and a significant reason for this has to do with social media. Online bullying, sexting, chat forums, the growing lack of sleep from being bombarded by communication well into the night, not to mention the impact of blue light from our devices on our bodies and the hollow narrative that our worth is now defined by how many likes or comments we get from whatever image or text we post: all this is now normal. If that were not enough, there is the constant need and pressure for us to show somehow that our life is packed with fun all the time and that it should be viewed and approved by whoever wants to be our friend, follower or groupie.

That is exhausting!

I have watched one of my own daughters face online bullying. It left her feeling lonely and deeply hurt by the comments and slurs made by many whom she considered to be her friends.

When we live with FOMO, the fear of missing out, turning off our devices is really difficult. But not only are we afraid we might miss out, we are in most cases addicted to our devices. People now have phantom sensations where they imagine their phone to be vibrating on their leg or think they have heard the noise of a notification. We live with a heightened expectation that we will be contacted, and check our devices repeatedly. We also seem to think it's okay to stop other people mid-flow in whatever they might be doing, to show them whatever it is we have just viewed online.

In our research, when we asked people what they thought had the most negative impact on their lives, the vast majority claimed it was social media. So the very thing that we do the most we also recognize causes us the greatest stress and personal challenge.

We need to take control of our devices!

We need to be so careful as to what we share about ourselves, whom we connect with, what we view and send, and how often we connect online. It doesn't need to be 24/7. In our house all devices are left downstairs and turned off after 8 p.m. That might sound weird, but my teenagers have discovered a freedom knowing that they can't be contacted after that time. We also need to be open about what we are sharing. Would you be comfortable if your parents were to read what you send or view? If not, does that tell you something? When we face problems such as bullying or being harassed, we need to tell someone who can help us deal with it. Don't suffer in silence, even if they have something on you. Speak up.

I am a big fan of social media, but without boundaries it will control us. Jesus does not want anything to control you; he wants you to live without the pressures of conformity and to be free of addiction. If social media causes you stress and pressure, then that is not the kind of relaxation God has in mind for you. It is time to take back control and create new boundaries.

Friends

When we moved back to live in the UK, after years abroad, my eldest daughter was in the sixth form and she sounded different from everyone else around her. She was a novelty. She quickly became friends with the main group who were popular and adventurous. However, it wasn't long before she became uncomfortable with this group. They were all pleasant enough, but there was one particular girl, whom I have called Tanya, who always sat alone. No one engaged with her. The group talked about Tanya behind her back and was generally unkind about her.

My daughter gravitated towards Tanya. She wanted to get to know her and to become her friend. It bothered her that she was alone and that others made fun of her.

Tanya opened up to her and shared her story. The previous year this girl had taken the entire school year off because she was pregnant, and against the advice of friends and family Tanya had the baby. It was a little boy. However, Tanya's baby was sick and the doctors informed her there was nothing they could do for him and he would die within just a few days. At just 17 years old, Tanya held the little boy for hour after hour in her hospital bed. A week after he was born, the baby died in her arms.

My daughter was filled with concern and compassion for the pain Tanya must have experienced. Upon reflection, she didn't need to be part of the big popular group. She wanted to be friends with someone who genuinely needed a friend.

We were created to be relational; we are wired to connect with other people; we were not designed to be alone but rather to enjoy friendships.

We need people in our lives whom we enjoy being around, who bring life and who look out for us. We need people we can be honest with, people we trust and people whom we can depend on. Relationships are God's gift to us! However, the Bible encourages us to choose our friends wisely (Prov. 12.26) and to recognize that a poor friendship can corrode our character (1 Cor. 15.33).

So let me ask you – whom do you trust? Which friend has your back? When was the last time someone who matters to you pulled you up for the way you acted, or was concerned over your behaviour? We need friends who will make us laugh and feel good, but these qualities have to be lower on the list than trust and concern for our well-being. We need friends who will speak truth into our lives. These are the things that matter in relationships.

Friendship has to be equal. The Bible reminds us that iron sharpens iron, so we should sharpen others (Prov. 27.17). In other words, by being around your friends, you should be better for it and so should they.

Friendships matter. If you are with people who do not have the same values as you, who do not respect what you believe and try to pull you away from living the way you feel that you should as a Christian, then they may not be the best friends for you to have. In any case, you should be pushing for the very best in them and wanting them always to do well. They should know that you care and can be trusted.

My daughter and Tanya became friends. While Tanya had different lifestyle values, she knew that my daughter cared for her, and it wasn't long before Tanya wanted to know more about her faith.

Your friends will help shape your character, your views on how you see the world, your habits and to some degree your beliefs. Be wise about whom you are surrounding yourself with and ensure they are people who care for you, people who enjoy being with you and who will encourage you to be a better person. If your current friends don't do that, consider reviewing who you spend time with and how much influence you allow people to have in your life.

God has designed you to have friends. Throughout the Bible we see people walking through life with close friends. You need friends, but be careful to surround yourself with the kind of friends who want the very best for you and encourage you all the way to achieving that.

Gaming or whatever your thing is

My first computer was a Commodore 64 and the games were loaded through a cassette player (tape). In today's terms it was prehistoric, embarrassingly so! I don't have a game console now. I just have my phone and iPad and download whatever I want to play within seconds.

When I am stressed, bored or just waiting for something, my phone is out and I escape into a digital world where I get to be the hero or compete online with some random person I will never meet. Which is usually a good thing, since I am trying to destroy that person in the game. Most of the time I lose, but that's mainly because someone decides to call me halfway through the game and my device shuts down whatever I am playing, automatically disqualifying me.

I don't know if gaming is your thing – it might be sports, dance, shopping, seeing a football match or something totally random. We all need our thing; we need to be able to shut down and escape. That's good! That's really important. So how much of your time do you really do that?

Some people simply don't do the 'me' thing enough, while others do it way too much. Doing what re-energizes you is critical, but it needs to be in balance. I remember playing a strategy game for two days solid. When I closed my eyes to go to sleep, all I could see was the graphics from the game. I even dreamt about it and, worse, in church when I closed my eyes for prayers the following morning I could still see the graphics! That was out of balance.

Let's find things that cause us to relax. Let's do things that give us life and energize us, but let's also make sure we get the rhythm of balance. We need to work or study, we need to help out around the house, we need to spend time with family, be involved in church stuff, as well as other things, but we also need the 'me' time. You were made to have it, so make sure you get it, but always within balance and rhythm.

Whether it be TV, social media, friends or gaming, ensure you get time to relax, but whatever you do needs to be appropriate and must not in any way conflict with your values and beliefs. Ultimately the way we spend our time should not harm our relationship with God but should either be neutral or draw us closer to him. Watching porn or playing games that make us really angry and frustrated will create barriers and be generally unhealthy for us.

Jesus cares what happens in our living room. He wants us to rest and relax, but let's include him in how that looks and let him be a part of reshaping things where our activities need some adjustments.

THE LIVING ROOM CHECKLIST:

⏲ WRITE UNDER EACH ACTIVITY HOW OFTEN YOU DO IT:

0–30 MINUTES PER WEEK

30–60 MINUTES PER WEEK

1–3 HOURS PER WEEK

3–6 HOURS PER WEEK

6 HOURS OR MORE PER WEEK

🚦THEN WRITE THE APPROPRIATE TRAFFIC LIGHT COLOUR:

GREEN – NO CONCERNS

AMBER – SOME CONCERNS

RED – SOME REAL ISSUES

FLASHING – HELP NEEDED NOW

TV (INCLUDING ON DEMAND)

⏲ _____

🚦 _____

YOUTUBE

⏲ _____

🚦 _____

MOVIES

⏲ _____

🚦 _____

SOCIAL MEDIA

🕐 _____

🚦 _____

SURFING THE WEB

🕐 _____

🚦 _____

HAVING FRIENDS OVER

🕐 _____

🚦 _____

GOING OUT WITH FRIENDS

🕐 _____

🚦 _____

GAMING

🕐 _____

🚦 _____

SPORTS

🕐 _____

🚦 _____

CLUB ACTIVITIES

🕐 _____

🚦 _____

CHURCH ACTIVITIES BY CHOICE

🕐 _____

🚦 _____

SHOPPING (AT STORES)

🕐 _____

🚦 _____

(OTHER) _____

🕐 _____

🚦 _____

(OTHER) _____

🕐 _____

🚦 _____

(OTHER) _____

🕐 _____

🚦 _____

AMBER
LIST THE ISSUES YOU'VE LABELLED AS AMBER
AND WHAT YOU NEED TO DO ABOUT THEM…

RED

LIST THE ISSUES YOU'VE LABELLED AS RED
AND WHAT YOU NEED TO DO ABOUT THEM...

FLASHING

LIST THE ISSUES YOU'VE LABELLED AS
FLASHING AND WHAT YOU NEED TO DO
ABOUT THEM...

7 DINING ROOM

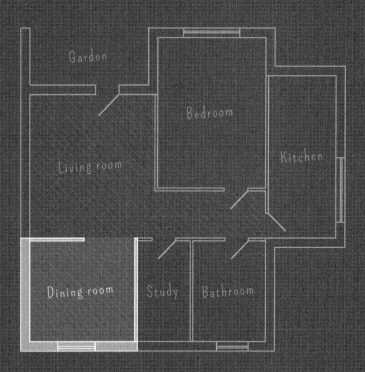

Hannah's day began like any other. It was a Friday. She fell out of bed, got ready for school and darted out of the door with her device. A lively 14-year-old, Hannah loved music.

When Hannah got home from school that day, her mum was out. She felt uneasy. Hannah hated being alone in the house with her mum's boyfriend. That afternoon, Hannah's worst fears came true – he tried to kiss her. She panicked and ran out of the house. It was the day everything changed.

Later that night, pleading and crying made no difference. Her mother just couldn't accept that it had happened. 'You're a liar, you've always hated him.' Hannah was stunned. Feeling desperate and abandoned, she ran away from home.

With no one to turn to, Hannah eventually moved in with a man twice her age.

Living with this man, Hannah hoped she had found a father figure who could make her feel loved. But when Hannah became pregnant, he threw her out.

By the time Youth for Christ youth workers met Hannah she was 17. Feeling that she had no choice, she had aborted the baby and was living with another older man.

Hannah had no self-esteem. She wore provocative clothes and make-up like a mask – to cover up years of pain. She longed for acceptance, but ended up feeling empty and used.

Immediately, the youth workers found her somewhere safe to stay. They began to talk to her about life. They learnt that Hannah's

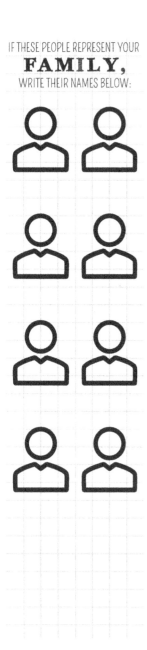

dad had walked out years ago. He wanted nothing to do with her – and she craved the love of a father.

Over the course of a year, Hannah began going to a church. She listened as they spoke about a heavenly Father whose love is pure and complete. She told one of the youth workers, 'I've tried everything. I've chased men, done drugs, drunk myself stupid . . . But you really believe in what you say. I'm willing to give Jesus a chance.'

One Sunday, Hannah had another life-changing day – she became a Christian. During a church service everything seemed to click into place. She asked the Youth for Christ youth worker to pray with her – and she hasn't looked back since: 'Now I really under-stand what it means to be loved.' (Hannah's story is taken from a YFC newsletter.)

Hannah had found a new family. She not only joined God's family by becoming his child, loved and cared for, but she became a member of a church family. Hannah's own family had fallen apart before she reached 14, but the story of her identity and belonging was far from over.

When Jesus walks into the dining room of your life, he isn't interested in what's on the menu (don't worry, he wants to know all about that when he steps into the kitchen). In the dining room, he wants to know who sits around the table, what the family you belong to is like and how that family works.

When I grew up, we didn't really sit around the table for dinner. I would eat my dinner on my knee while watching TV. I know some families that never really eat together at all but gulp their food down while racing out of the kitchen to their next activity. This room, however, is about your community.

Family is a very big deal in the Bible. Your family describes your identity and who you belong to. It would be fair to say that God is very big on family and created it to be the centrepiece of our lives and critical to community.

So, what is your family like?

Perhaps it was like mine? Traditional, biological mum and dad, together with brothers and sisters.

Equally it could be just a mum or a dad and any siblings. It could even be mum and mum, or dad and dad.

However, it is just as likely to be one biological parent with a step-parent and either half-siblings or a blended family with children unrelated to you in the house.

If that doesn't describe your family set-up then perhaps your parents had the incredible privilege of choosing you and you are adopted, living with parents who love you just as much as any biological parent could.

If none of the above fit then perhaps you are living with relatives, such as grandparents? For some, you may be fostered or children who live in communities with other children. This list is by no means exhaustive.

Families can be messy, and today families are defined far more by where you belong rather than by your DNA.

For some, though, that sense of belonging (or lack of it?) can be painful. For Hannah, her biological family setting was very messy and resulted in a lot of pain.

For others, family is a place of warmth, love and safety.

As Jesus walks into your dining room and explores your family setting, he deeply cares about how you feel, what it looks like and the role you play within your family context.

Families at best are loving, safe and secure places to be; at worst they are dysfunctional and broken with pain and rejection. Most families have elements of both – love is foundational, but how that love is expressed is not always so obvious and can be at times confusing. The truth is the vast majority of parents and guardians are doing the best they can. There is no school on parenting and the only example most people have is their own upbringing, which most likely was flawed.

In our research we asked people just like you to tell us about their families. When we asked who they wanted to spend most time with, families came bottom of the list – no big surprise. However, when we asked who they most wanted to please in life, families came top of the list by far. Within all of us is a desire to belong and to please those who care for us. In a broken world, that can get messy. I would suggest, however, that in the overwhelming majority of cases those who are responsible for raising us love us deeply (even if they don't always say it). Families matter very much to the vast majority of people, including you.

Take a moment and consider a few questions regarding your family:

- When are you happiest at home?
- When do you laugh the most, and what do you laugh about?

- What are your favourite moments?
- When do you feel most safe?
- When do you feel most loved and valued?

It won't take long for most of us to have many positive thoughts flooding into our minds, with a realization that home and family is a good and healthy community, while recognizing also that it isn't always perfect.

If, however, home for whatever reason isn't safe and you live in fear, then you need to tell a person of responsibility, such as a pastor, youth worker, teacher, social worker or, depending on how bad things are, quite possibly the police. Home should never be a place you feel unsafe, and you have a basic right to be safe.

If your context is safe and generally warm then you have a role to play in the way your family works. You get to be a positive voice and a constructive player in the family team.

God is big on relationships. At the very start of the Bible, he says that a man will leave his mother and father and be united to his wife and the two will become one. In other words, a man and a woman will marry, have sex and, if able, at some point start a family. We know children are high on the agenda because God instructs couples to 'multiply.' To be clear, God means 'make little people'. He wants us to start families and grow communities. That said, children are not for everyone. That is more than okay, and for lots of healthy reasons people have reached that decision. Within most people, though, is an inbuilt desire to have children at some stage in life and start their own small community that will belong to a bigger community. Needless to say, there are of course couples who desperately want to have children but struggle to do so, which becomes a painful journey and there is a need to be sensitive to that. In the main, family is part of God's structure for us and society.

Below are just a few things God has to say to adults:

10
9
8
7
6
5
4
3
2
1

1 Form a relationship, have children and create a family (Gen. 1.28; 2.24).
2 Parents need to look after and care for their families (1 Tim. 5.8).
3 Families need to place God at the very centre of everything (Josh. 24.15).
4 Parents need to teach children about life and what is good (Prov. 22.6).
5 Parents should love their children and not exasperate them (Eph. 6.4).

That all seems pretty good stuff. God has lots more to say on what parenting should look like and how children should be cared for and loved. He is absolutely for you!

If you were to mark your family on points 2–5 I don't know what grades you would give out of 10, but hopefully home is a very safe and caring place. If it isn't, then again I want to encourage you to chat to someone who can hear your story and speak to whether that's really okay or not and then provide positive and constructive help.

God, however, also has a few expectations on how you should be within your family. Are you ready for this?

1 Honour your mum and dad (or your carers) (Exod. 20.12).
2 Obey your mum and dad's (carer's) instructions today (Col. 3.20).

3 Live by the guidance, teaching and advice your mum and dad (carers) provided you with in life (Prov. 6.20).

4 Try to please your parents (carers) (Prov. 15.20).

5 Respect your mum and dad (carers) (Deut. 5.16).

There is a fairly strong theme here: honour, obey, follow, please and respect your mum and dad (carers). That isn't always going to fill you with happiness, nor is it always going to be something you want to do. If your parents or carers were to mark you on 1–5, what grades might they give?

God's family code goes like this: parents, you need to love, care for, teach and protect your children; children, you need to offer respect, do as you are told and try to please your parents. There is also a further code: each member of the family needs to place God at the centre of everything!

Being part of a family does not make you a passenger on a bus. It is not an 18-year journey where you are just filling in time, waiting to get to your destination so you can get off the bus and live your own life. In other words, you don't get to be done with family at 18! In God's structure and with his code, there is a much bigger plan. You have a role to play under 18 and you have a similar role to play over 18. God is not a fan of individualism, but of community. He created you to belong, and belonging means receiving, contributing and following the code.

The problem is that family is messy.

My family didn't go to church, so when I became a Christian I was the only one who had to work out what it meant to put God first, not only for me but also within a family context. So, if your family doesn't live out their faith, or even have one, what does it look like to put God first within family?

ANTICIPATED GRADE

10 9 8 7 6 5 4 3 2 1

There is still a way to do that, and following God's instructions on how we are to do our part becomes key.

Some parents have hurt us and broken the family home. What does it mean to love and respect a parent who split up the family and barely wants anything to do with those left behind?

There is still a way to do that, and following God's instructions on how we are to do our part becomes key.

Some parents or carers have their own struggles and may have addictions or mental health challenges, which makes following their instructions and obeying them really confusing and difficult at times. If their requests are unhealthy or dangerous, then we obviously can't and must not do anything to cause harm or fudge around laws. Sharing your context with other adults is essential, but there may be aspects where . . .

There is still a way to do that (which pursues health and positive boundaries), and following God's instructions on how we are to do our part becomes key.

For some, the level of mess has been too great and home has not been a healthy place. For reasons of safety, families have been forcibly split – there are no words of comfort that will ease the pain of that situation. That is not the way God intended family to be, and that is not the best that God had in store. However, we still belong within God's family; we are still loved and very much wanted.

For the majority, families (however they may look) are quirky with both rough edges and smooth surfaces. Working out how we apply God's desired code for living individually and as a community is very important.

As Jesus walks into your dining room, where are the changes needed?

Is it perhaps in the way in which you communicate with your parents (carers)? Or is it the reality that you might not always do what they ask? Do you show respect towards them, or is your tone and general response more disrespectful?

How you respond matters to Jesus. A change in how you talk, act and respond in general could make a profound difference to how your parents (carers) talk, act and respond to you as well. We are called to contribute regardless of our age and position within the family. Family matters, and God asks and expects us to work hard at making family a positive and valued feature within our lives. We have our part to play.

WHERE DO YOU NEED TO ALLOW JESUS TO MAKE ADJUSTMENTS IN YOUR FAMILY SETTING?

SCORE EACH AREA OUT OF 10 AND WRITE HOW YOU WILL MAKE IMPROVEMENTS:

TIME I SPEND WITH FAMILY

_____
_____
_____

QUALITY OF ATTENTION THAT I GIVE TO MY FAMILY

_____
_____
_____

THE WAY I TALK TO MY FAMILY MEMBERS

_____
_____
_____

THE LEVEL AT WHICH I LISTEN TO MY FAMILY

_____
_____
_____

ACTING ON WHAT IS ASKED OF ME BY PARENTS/CARERS

_____
_____
_____

THE WAY IN WHICH I SHOW KINDNESS TO MY FAMILY MEMBERS

_____
_____
_____

THE WAY IN WHICH I GENERALLY CONDUCT
MYSELF AROUND FAMILY

_____
_____
_____

KEEPING MY PART OF THE BARGAIN (CLEANING
ROOM/CHORES ETC.)

_____
_____
_____

TALKING ABOUT MY FAMILY IN A RESPECTFUL
WAY WITH OTHERS

_____
_____
_____

MY LEVEL OF ENCOURAGEMENT AND
ENGAGEMENT ON SPIRITUAL MATTERS (CHURCH,
PRAYER ETC.) WITH THE FAMILY

_____
_____
_____

HOW QUICKLY I AM WILLING TO RESOLVE
PROBLEMS, DISAGREEMENTS AND HURT WITH
ALL FAMILY MEMBERS

_____
_____
_____

8 KITCHEN

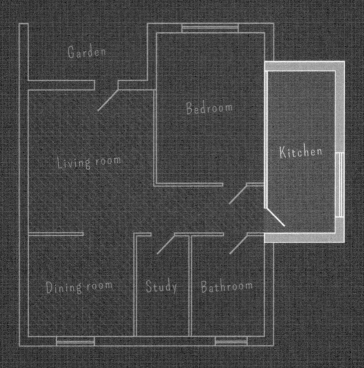

If Jesus walked into my kitchen, I am not sure how often he would find me there! I have an aversion to that room. I love food, but I don't like cooking, and I hate washing the dishes. All I want to do is eat out all of the time. I crave fast food, junk and pretty much any kind of convenience eating.

The kitchen represents so much more than preparing and cleaning up food – it represents health. My diet has been anything but healthy in the past. However, I am not getting any younger and when I decided recently to climb the world's tallest freestanding mountain (Kilimanjaro) to raise funds for Youth for Christ, I realized that change was required. What I ate and how much I exercised suddenly became the centre of attention, not just for me or for my wife, but also for people at work who became intrigued as to whether I really could change the habits of a lifetime.

The kitchen represents the health of our very being.

Before you skip this chapter as irrelevant or as holding no real interest, let me tell you a secret: Jesus as a teenager had to find balance to his life as well. Health was just as much an issue for him. Even though he was fully God, he was also fully human, which meant he would have had his own version of tasty junk food to snack on. We get a hint of that in the Bible where it says, 'Jesus grew in wisdom and stature, and in favour with God and man' (Luke 2.52, NIV). In other words, Jesus grew mentally, physically, socially and spiritually as a teenager. Jesus found balance; he found a healthy way of living.

So the awkward question is this: would you describe your life as healthy? By your life I mean your diet and exercise, but I also mean your habits, your study, your friendships and your connection with God. Are they in balance or would you say they are a little lopsided?

Take a look at the diagram of the wheel of life. Mark for each category how strong you believe you are: 1 is weak and 5 is strong. Then connect all of the categories together to give you an idea of how balanced your current pattern of living might be.

How balanced is your wheel of life? Is it in a perfect circle, or is it a little lopsided in parts? Don't worry if it is all over the place; you are not alone.

I was recently climbing rocks with one of my teenage daughters. We stood on a sizeable rock overlooking another rock no more than 15 metres tall and watched a father with two small children trying to climb down. With a few scrapes and tight moments they all made it to the bottom. The younger boy shouted out, 'That was dangerously awesome!' The adrenaline and euphoria of climbing down what appeared to that child to be a risky challenge had overwhelmed him as he bounced around with excitement celebrating their achievement. He was ecstatic and looked to our rock as his next adventure.

There was something about that comment that stayed with me. What does it mean to live

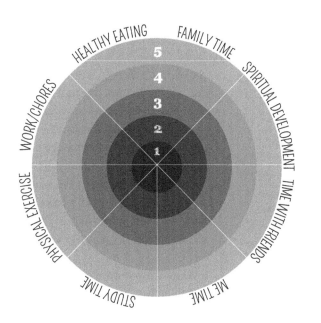

HEALTHY EATING
FAMILY TIME
SPIRITUAL DEVELOPMENT
TIME WITH FRIENDS
ME TIME
STUDY TIME
PHYSICAL EXERCISE
WORK/CHORES

5
4
3
2
1

a dangerously awesome life? We are made for adventure – some more than others, but within all of us is the desire to conquer, to achieve something significant and overcome risk.

I wonder, though, whether the fear of missing out (FOMO) has replaced our desire for adventure. While on the rocks, I watched my daughter check her phone multiple times. She was visibly torn between the desire to climb and overcome some sizeable obstacles and the desire to check in to see what others were doing and whether she might be missing out. She was struggling to live in the moment and conquer the adventure before her. The little boy, whom we watched scrambling down a much smaller rock than the one we happened to be on, did not have a phone and had not yet discovered social media nor the pressures of checking in. Instead, he wanted to live a dangerously awesome life.

Part of a healthy life is to have healthy boundaries.

There are times to check in with our friends, but there are also times to be free from the thoughts of missing out. We need to enjoy

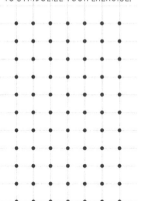

our own adventures. We can't, nor should we, live in a constant state of adrenaline rush, but there should be enough moments when we can push ourselves to explore and enjoy life in a safe setting without the fear of missing out on what others might be doing. It isn't just those adrenaline moments that we need. We also need moments of being alone, watching a movie, reading a book – whatever helps to recharge the batteries of life.

Although we need to eat in a balanced way, that doesn't mean we can't occasionally enjoy something that is so incredibly tasty and shockingly calorific that we desperately look forward to it. If we only ate junk then it would quickly affect the quality of our lives. While I may want to eat out all the time, I really don't (though you will struggle to find me in the kitchen – not because I don't help out around the house, but because I don't like this room). Age, budget and common sense are dictating my habits. Balance is important. God has given us bodies in which to live this life, and our bodies are fragile and need taking care of.

As a teenager I was pretty good at martial arts. I fought at county and national level and I went on to attend a sports college where you could only get in if you were at a highly competitive level. I trained an average of four hours every day. I was obsessed with being as fit as possible. As soon as I took up youth work, my exercise dropped remarkably, the pounds came on and it wasn't until I set myself the challenge of climbing Kilimanjaro that I started to work at getting back into shape. I have to confess that I am nowhere near as fit as I was at 18 (I am not even sure that is possible). Off the back of climbing a mountain, I realized I still needed to keep in reasonable shape, which has resulted in my getting a dog. Two long walks a day keeps me moving.

I'm saying all this from personal experience. I struggle to exercise, but I have come to realize I need to. I recognize that if I don't look after this fragile body of mine then things will start to break. Exercise is important, not only for our physical but also for our mental well-being. The more we exercise the sharper our minds become and the healthier our emotions feel, and, needless to say, the longer our hearts should last.

What are you doing to exercise? Figure out what works for you! You won't find me doing more than a fast walk, which is in total contrast to when I was 18. Back then I was kicking and punching to stay fit. If sport is not your thing, there are lots of other ways to stay healthy, some already covered in other chapters, such as family time. Some we have yet to cover, such as our time spent with God.

The wheel of life showed you areas that you might need to focus on, and areas where you are strong. You get one life here on earth, and God wants you to live and experience it to the full. I am not sure our lives should be dangerously awesome, but we need to push for experiences. Not all our experiences will be enjoyable, but they should be varied. Honestly, every time I eat a Brussels sprout it is far from awesome, but my body appreciates it nevertheless. Sitting in a room checking my phone every five minutes to see who has posted what, or what message I may or may not have received, is an energy drain that leaves me feeling as though I have lost an entire day. In truth I have: I have conquered little and lived a day out of balance. Each time you take time out to study, you might be missing out on other more tempting things, but your brain is better for it. Taking

AND JESUS GREW IN
**WISDOM
AND STATURE,**
AND IN FAVOUR WITH
**GOD AND
MAN.**
(LUKE 2.52, NIV)

time to pray rather than being online will reap a powerful spiritual return in the long run.

Variety and balance are key to healthy living.

The question then is: what do you need to focus on in order to create a healthy balance across your life?

Since 94 per cent of young people are online daily, and the average teenager spends up to five hours online each day, I suspect connecting with friends and possibly 'me time' may take a fairly sizeable chunk out of your overall time (if you are like the vast majority of your friends).

As a teenager Jesus found perfect balance mentally, physically, socially and spiritually (Luke 2.52). What would it take for you to find greater balance in your life?

When Jesus walks into the kitchen of your life, he wants to help you understand what a balanced life should look like for you. Changes here may mean addressing some deep-rooted patterns and habits. The only way we can change a habit is by identifying it and admitting that some habits in our lives have become unhealthy and out of balance, while other important areas may have been neglected altogether.

Just as there are plants in your kitchen, some of which have dried up and died, out of neglect, while others are wild and chaotic and in desperate need of pruning, so there will almost certainly be things in your life that need attention and things that may need to be reduced.

Will you allow Jesus to help you identify and work on each of those areas?

A BALANCED LIFE UNDER REVIEW:

HEALTHY EATING

IS IT HEALTHY? _____

WHAT DO I NEED TO DO? _____

_____

_____

FAMILY TIME

IS IT HEALTHY? _____

WHAT DO I NEED TO DO? _____

_____

_____

SPIRITUAL DEVELOPMENT

IS IT HEALTHY? _____

WHAT DO I NEED TO DO? _____

_____

_____

TIME WITH FRIENDS

IS IT HEALTHY? _____

WHAT DO I NEED TO DO? _____

_____

_____

'ME' TIME

IS IT HEALTHY? _____

WHAT DO I NEED TO DO? _____

_____

_____

STUDY TIME

IS IT HEALTHY? _____

WHAT DO I NEED TO DO? _____

_____

_____

PHYSICAL EXERCISE

IS IT HEALTHY? _____

WHAT DO I NEED TO DO? _____

_____

_____

WORK/CHORES

IS IT HEALTHY? _____

WHAT DO I NEED TO DO? _____

_____

_____

9 STUDY

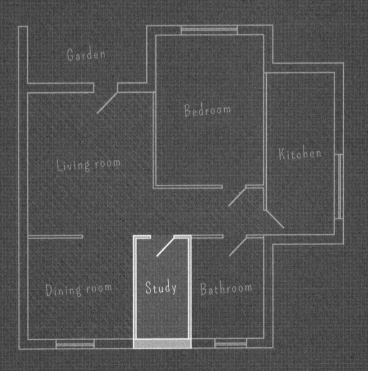

Garden

Bedroom

Kitchen

Living room

Dining room

Study

Bathroom

If you walked into my house, it wouldn't take you very long to figure out that there isn't a study – it is just too small a building to have one. You would instead find a desk with a computer on it in the front room, with a bookshelf full of random books next to the desk. But it hardly passes as a study!

I don't know if your house has a study, but your metaphorical house certainly does. When Jesus walks into that room, he will want to know not only what happens in there but what books you have on the shelf and how you use your time whenever you are in that room to grow.

Perhaps you don't spend much time in the study at all. The bookshelf may have a thick layer of dust on it, while the desk is piled high with junk that is yet to find a proper home elsewhere. You barely step into this room at all.

On the other hand, you might be in there daily. You want to grow, so you read; but you also write, reflect and journal. What's more, you love to sit and look out of the window and get lost in your thoughts. I have no idea how you might use this room.

This room, though, is far more than just a room for learning: it is a room that reflects your relationship with God. The study is about connecting and growing in your faith and beliefs; it is a place to strengthen the core of your being with the Creator of the universe. The study is perhaps the most sacred and holy place in your house. It is a place where you meet with God in your own unique way. It is a place where he waits for you.

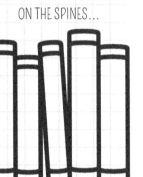

When I first became a Christian, I was told that you had to pray and read your Bible each day – that time was called a 'quiet time'. Each Christian should spend one hour a day having a quiet time. The reason I was told it should be one hour is because when Jesus was about to be arrested in the garden, he spent time praying but kept finding that the disciples who were with him had fallen asleep. When he woke them up, he asked, 'Can't you spend at least one hour praying?' So arose the notion that all Christians should spend one hour a day in prayer.

For the first 18 months I prayed every day for an hour. I found it hard and I would often fall asleep (just like the disciples). It became a rigid activity – something I must do. I watched the clock tick down whenever I was having my quiet time and every day I approached my one hour with a sense of duty, and, if I'm honest, I also dreaded it just a little. If I ever missed it, or I cut the time short, I felt really guilty. But for one hour every day I would find a room (usually my bedroom), close the door and start the clock.

How do you pray? What does your Bible reading look like? What other books do you read to help you grow?

I remember hearing one of my youth leaders saying, 'Try to pray for at least 15 minutes every day, but if you really can't do that at least give God five minutes!' I was shocked. Who was I to try and give God five minutes?! The Bible said an hour, so it needed to be an hour! There was an element of religious pride to my reaction.

While I certainly approached my quiet time with a sense of sacrifice and commitment, and some good old religious enthusiasm, I was missing the point entirely.

There is a verse in the Bible that confused me. It says, 'pray . . . on all occasions' (Eph. 6.18, NIV). How could I pray on all occasions? Surely I just had to pray for an hour each day. I couldn't pray for 24 hours every day.

I then heard of a famous preacher who was quoted as saying that he never prayed for more than 15 minutes at a time, but 15 minutes never went by without him praying. In a sense, he prayed all the time. While he was awake he was in and out of prayer.

I came to realize that my relationship with God should not involve a clock, but, rather like all relationships, it needs to be natural and fluid. The study is a room that we should be in and out of continually. Since prayer is about developing our connection with God, like all relationships it needs to be prioritized and worked on.

There was a man in the Bible called Enoch. We don't know very much about him, other than that he walked with God and God loved him.

I want to be like Enoch. My relationship with God has a great deal of room for improvement, but I've personally abandoned the long solitary approach to prayer and changed it to something far more fluid.

Before I even get out of bed, as I begin to stir, and usually before I have opened my eyes, I have trained myself to move my fading dreams to thoughts on God. While I am waking up I usually think of who he is (the Creator of the universe, the Lord of my life, my heavenly Dad) and then I welcome him into my day and hand it over to him for him to lead and own. I do that because I read in the Bible that I need to seek the things of God first in my life (Matt. 6.33). So while I am waking up, just thinking about him is one such way I can try to seek him.

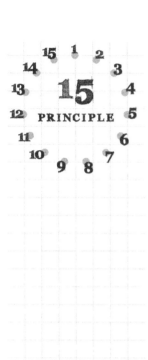

15

PRINCIPLE

Then I jump out of bed, use the loo and head downstairs to make a coffee. After that I pop back up to bed and read my Bible, which is a set reading. (There are lots of Bible reading guides out there to help us – try 'Mettle' by Youth for Christ if you don't have one.) I then work on a simple format. I thank God for what he has done in my life (maybe reflecting on the previous day). I then ask him for help with things coming up and pray for people and situations needing help. I also bring to mind my mistakes and ask for forgiveness. That might take me ten minutes.

I then get dressed and head to work.

My mind, though, is in and out of praying for people and things throughout the day. I make notes of things and situations that need prayer and will often go back to them at a later point. Some days I may be in and out of prayer thoughts a dozen or more times, whereas other days it may only be two or three times.

At some point in the day I also try to read a Christian book to help me think more about my faith and stretch my existing understanding. I might only read a page, or I might get to read a chapter. The fact that you are reading this book indicates you also are doing that. There are so many great books to stretch and encourage us.

While that might sound prescriptive, there is a lot of movement in my prayer time.

Some days, all I manage is to think on God as I wake up and find a few times in the day to reflect more on him. Other days, I cram in lots of prayer activities. There is, however, no guilt over what I fail to achieve but rather an excitement to find the time; and if I don't, then I don't. God still loves me just as much and waits for me to join him the next day.

So in reality I am in and out of the study room. Sometimes I might enter for no more than ten seconds as I reflect on a thought, while at other times I could be there for ten minutes as I really press into prayer.

My point here is simple. Everyone has ideas on how their prayer times should be. I came to the conclusion that there is no formula, there is no one-size-fits-all, but rather God made you and me unique, and therefore the way in which we connect with God will be unique for each of us. If blocking out a certain amount of time works for you and helps you grow, then that is fantastic; if, however, it is more fluid and that works, then again that is fantastic.

Jesus got up every day before it was light to pray, but he also prayed throughout the day in lots of ways: he read the Scriptures and reflected on the things of God continually. Prayer was central to everything.

So while I want to encourage you to figure out your own unique prayer space and approach, the main point to make is that it is important to connect with God and read the Bible. We were designed to meet with God and to connect with him. Whenever we do, he brings life to our souls and strengthens our relationship with him.

I once heard a story of a young monk who lived in a monastery. After a few years he approached the abbot (senior monk) to inform him that he did not feel any closer to God than when he first arrived. The abbot listened and suggested that the young monk spend a few years living as a hermit (on his own) in a cave many miles from the monastery. The monk agreed and headed out to live on his own in pursuit of growing closer to God. After five years the abbot paid the young monk a visit in his cave and asked him if he was now any closer to God. The younger monk replied that he wasn't. The abbot reflected for a moment and instructed the monk to follow him. They walked into the wilderness for three days and, when they were approaching a river, the abbot told the monk to look at his reflection in the water. The monk obliged, and studied his image, one he had not seen for some time. He had aged and had a wild beard, but other than that he looked somewhat the same. The abbot then instructed the monk to move closer to the water and rest his nose on the surface of the water. The monk did as he was told, but without any warning the abbot came from behind and pushed the monk's head under the water. A fight developed where the monk desperately tried to raise his head out of the water but the abbot was stronger and had the more dominant position. After some time, the monk became weaker and eventually stopped struggling – he was now drowning. At that point the abbot pulled the monk out of the water and tossed his limp body aside. As the air hit the young monk's lungs he immediately started to cough and gasp. After a few moments the monk looked in disbelief and concern at the abbot and asked him why he had tried to kill him, to which the abbot replied, 'Until you pant for God in the same way you crave for oxygen you will never be satisfied!' The lesson was understood in an instant.

The most common desire I hear from other Christians is to improve their prayer lives. We shouldn't be dissatisfied by how we pray, but rather at our lack of desire to connect with God. Prayer is simply the tool. I learnt a long time ago that we prioritize and commit to that which we desire the most. How much do you really desire to connect with God? That desire needs to be matched by our commitment to seek him whatever that might look like or whatever the cost.

The author of Psalm 42 puts it this way: 'As the deer pants for streams of water, so my soul pants for you, my God' (Ps. 42.1, NIV). Without water we die of thirst, but with it we are energized and it gives us life. Praying connects us to God, who satisfies our innermost being because we were created to know him.

During some prayer times, I feel as if I have really connected with God, while at other times it feels as if I have been talking to myself. Prayer is not about feelings but about habits that form our relationship with him. So, whether we feel inspired to pray or not, we need to develop patterns and form our own disciplines that work uniquely for us to connect with God. In this way, we can grow in God and, just like Enoch, journey with him.

If you are uncertain about how to pray, and when people talk about it you just feel guilty, let me reassure you it doesn't need to be like that. There are lots of ways we can pray. Here are just a few:

1 *Conversations*. Spend time talking to God. It can be a chat in your head or out loud. If you are not sure how to do that, then perhaps base it on my own approach of saying 'Thank you' and making a list of things you might be grateful for, then moving to 'Please', where you ask God for things that you need and people you know, or things in the news that are in need of God's help. I would also suggest that you include 'Sorry': spend time asking God to forgive

you for things you may not have got right and that might be opposite to the way he wants you to live. This will prevent them becoming a barrier between you and God. He wants us to have clean hearts, and asking for forgiveness does just that.

2 *Journal.* In a blank book you may want to write out your prayers rather than say them (the above framework could work for you), but also reflect on thoughts that God is bringing to mind and map out the journey that you may be having in life and with God within the book. Journals work really well if you don't have the private space to be able to pray, so writing in public allows you to disappear and for everything around you to fade away as you communicate with God through pen and paper or on your device.

3 *Music and activity.* I have a set playlist on my device with worship songs that help me reflect on God, so on some days I abandon my normal approach, put on my earphones and go for a walk reflecting on him, and I bring the words of the songs into my daily situations and challenges. It works just as well in the car or in a coffee shop. If things in my life are turbulent, then listening to songs that speak into storms, or of his greatness, not only provides comfort but becomes a prayer as I claim that over my life. Equally, worship songs on

God's goodness and faithfulness can help us escape and focus on him no matter what may be happening in life.

4 *The Lord's Prayer*. Jesus specifically taught his disciples how to pray. We call it the Lord's Prayer. It goes like this:

> Our Father in heaven,
> hallowed be your name.
> Your kingdom come,
> your will be done on earth
> as it is in heaven.
> Give us this day our daily bread.
> Forgive us our sins as we forgive those
> who have sinned against us.
> Lead us not into temptation
> but deliver us from evil.

You may already know it! Many churches pray that prayer each Sunday across their church services. However, I would suggest that rather than reciting the prayer, you use it as a framework and you pray into each line, reflecting on what it says and how to apply it to your life. For example, when you pray, 'Our Father in heaven, blessed (hallowed) be your name', you might want to think of other names of God. 'God, I thank you that you are my Father, but you are also the King of Kings, you are the Maker of all things.' You could spend a few minutes just thinking about his names. When you get to 'give us this day our daily bread', you might list all the things that you need or would like to ask God for that day. Taking the Lord's Prayer line by line should springboard us into a time of focused prayer.

5 *Reflective prayer*. Another way you might pray is by taking well-known prayers or passages from the Bible and repeating the prayer or verse over and over, but emphasizing certain words progressively and reflecting on what that might mean. So, for

example, take the blind man who shouted out to Jesus, 'Jesus, Son of David, have mercy on me a sinner.' That is not a long quote, but it can become a very powerful prayer. You could repeat the prayer five times and each time emphasize a different part, reflecting on what it means to place an emphasis on 'Jesus' (who is he to you?), 'Son of David' (what does it mean to be the Son of David? who was David? what was the blind man acknowledging by saying that to Jesus?), 'Have mercy' (in what areas of your life do you need mercy?), 'on me' (specifically recognizing you need Jesus), 'a sinner' (what does it mean to be a sinner and how can Jesus bring about change?). As crazy as it sounds, I can be lost in prayer over this verse for 20 minutes, just reflecting on it. It doesn't need to be this verse; it can be anything that stimulates both thought and prayer. Another verse might be, 'Lord Jesus, I am not worthy to receive you, but only say the word and I shall be healed.' Or, 'I lift my eyes up to the mountains. Where does my help come from? It comes from the Lord, the maker of heaven and earth.' There are many verses one can use for such approaches.

6 *Art.* My wife Joy will often draw a picture or paint to express her worship. Other people I know dance and express themselves that way to God. I am not wired

that way at all, so that approach will never work for me, but I know of others who build things and make shapes that they connect to issues that need prayer. If drawing or dancing or expressing yourself in other artistic ways allows you to connect directly with God, then go for it!

7 *Silence.* Find a place where you can relax. You may want to sit or even lie down, but in the silence ask God to fill your thoughts with him. Try reading a Bible passage first and allow him to speak to you. Resist the urge to talk or do something else, but instead invite God to bring to your attention the things that he wants to speak to you about. I find my mind will sometimes wander when I am sitting in silence, but this can be important too. The people or things that come to mind may be issues I need to pray about or reflect further on. Sometimes, I need to dismiss those thoughts, empty my mind afresh and ask the Holy Spirit to speak to me once more. A young prophet in the Bible called Samuel prayed, 'Speak, Lord, your servant is listening.' Perhaps you could pray that as you enter a period of silence?

8 *The alphabet.* When I am struggling to form my thoughts and prayers, or I am distracted by other things, I will often work through the alphabet and use each letter to describe an issue for prayer. For example, A = awesome: 'God, you are so awesome and I am so in awe of you'; B = brave: 'Lord, I need to be brave for you in the situation I am facing today'; C = complete: 'Lord, you make me complete and today I need you'. X and Y can be a challenge!

Prayer does not need to be static or a one-size-fits-all approach. It certainly doesn't need to be boring. Rather, it should be life-giving. It should be done regularly so that we can connect and strengthen our relationship with God continually.

Prayer is so much more than asking. It is coming into God's presence to worship him, seek him and be reminded of who he is. It is walking through life with him. We must remember with prayer that

OUT OF THESE SUGGESTED
WAYS TO PRAY, WHICH ONE…
EXCITES YOU?

CONFUSES YOU?

WOULD STRETCH YOU?

WOULD HELP YOU?

God does not exist for our needs but rather we exist to serve him. So, while I may have needs, how might my prayers reflect the reality that I have also been created to please and serve God?

Be sure to read the Bible. There are many reading guides out there. If you are starting out, then let me encourage you to read one chapter of the Gospel of Mark and one chapter of the Psalms each day. The psalmist said, 'Your word [God's Bible] is a lamp to my feet and a light to my path' (Ps. 119.105, NASB). In other words, it is our guide through life. There are lots of ways to go about reading the Bible. The Bible is not just rich in teaching but has powerful stories of drama, war, mystery, revenge, love, murder, suspense, adventure and forgiveness. It is packed with plots and powerful revelations of who God is. There are also parts in the Bible that are difficult to understand, and without guides to unpack the original meaning we might be left confused and uncertain or even get the wrong idea. When that happens, ask someone or, dare I even say, do an internet search for the passage in question with the word 'commentary' next to it.

I also want to encourage you to read other Christian books so that you can be stretched and encouraged in your faith. What you believe, and knowing why you believe it, is really important. Understanding your beliefs creates an important foundation to faith when the storms, doubts, opposing questions and difficult experiences of life come your way.

Connecting with God does not need to be a dull task. Rather, over time, it can become a habit that brings life. It doesn't need to be one approach. I have given you eight ideas, but in truth there are so many more ways to pray and reflect and build your relationship with God.

The study is perhaps the only room where Jesus does not ask permission to come in and make changes: he is already there, waiting for you to join him. The Bible says that our bodies are a temple of the Holy Spirit. The moment you became a Christian God took up residence. However, as this book seeks to explore, Jesus does not wish to remain confined to the study but wishes to be part of every area of our lives.

Start at your own pace, even if that pace is taking one minute to acknowledge who God is, and inviting him to join you in your day. We all need to start somewhere, but hopefully your prayer life will be like all relationships – important, varied and fluid.

Jesus waits for you today. May your times with him be the most powerful experiences that you ever have.

WHAT DOES PRAYER LOOK LIKE FOR YOU?

ON A SCALE OF 1–10, HOW IMPORTANT IS PRAYER TO YOU?

___ / **10**

ON A SCALE OF 1–10, HOW MUCH OF A PRIORITY DO YOU MAKE IT?

___ / **10**

ON A SCALE OF 1–10, HOW EASY DO YOU FIND PRAYER?

___ / **10**

ON A SCALE OF 1–10, HOW VARIED ARE YOUR PRAYER TIMES?

___ / **10**

BASED ON YOUR ANSWERS ABOVE, WHAT, IF ANY, IMPROVEMENTS DO YOU NEED TO MAKE WHEN IT COMES TO PRAYER?

_____

_____

_____

_____

_____

10 BATHROOM

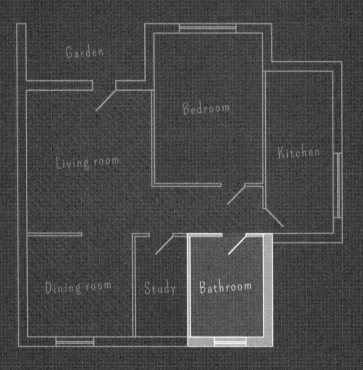

I remember playing with an old cassette recording device that belonged to my dad when I was about seven years old. I recorded stupid things and played them back. I doubt my dad would have been over-impressed by my jokes and giggles, especially as I most likely recorded over his own important work messages to himself. What surprised me, though, was the fact that I sounded different from how I would hear myself. I was convinced that I didn't sound like that, and the device was low quality. My only problem, however, was that my sister who was messing around with me sounded exactly the same (recorded or not). So how could that be?

When Jesus walks into the bathroom of your life, hygiene (while very important) is not his primary concern. Nor is how often you go to the toilet (again it's important). It's the mirror that has Jesus' attention. How often you use it and how you view the person in the reflection has his interest. Hygiene is in a sense an outworking of how you see yourself, but for Jesus there are issues about your identity and image that may need some attention.

So, how I heard myself on the recorder and how I heard my voice in everyday life were not the same. In reality, my voice sounds different to me from how it does to other people. For many people, the way they view themselves and the beliefs they hold about who they are and how important they may be are usually different from how others see them.

In Chapter 4 (Walls) we looked at the fact that our identity is often caught up in our image and how people see us, and that we need instead to be more concerned with how Jesus sees us.

WRITE THREE THINGS
THAT YOU SEE WHEN YOU
**LOOK IN
THE MIRROR:**

1

2

3

In the bathroom of our lives, by looking in the mirror we need to see the labels that people and situations have placed on our lives and how those labels shape how we see both ourselves and the world. What's more, we need to find ways to wash those negative labels off once and for all.

There are a few powerful forces out there that shape how we view ourselves: rejection, guilt and shame.

A running consideration throughout this book has been two universal questions, 'Who am I?' and 'Do I matter?' We have answered these questions in lots of ways, but if there are labels deeply interwoven into your life that consist of rejection, guilt or shame then I suspect you will have a hard time either with yourself or with other people. That will be in part because your answers to 'Who am I?' and 'Do I matter?' will struggle to reconcile the past with the present.

You may be a child of God and someone who does matter, deeply, but if something happened to you, or you have done something that you can't move on from, being a child of God may seem a secondary message in your life rather than a primary one. Again, we looked at both guilt and shame in Chapter 3 (Windows), but we can understand something theoretically without knowing how to allow it to bring about change.

The bathroom is the place to take a good hard look and ask, 'Okay, I may have grasped that I am loved by God and valued by him, and that my past has been dealt with, but do I still carry labels from my past that I can't get rid of and that shape how I see myself and others?'

For most of my life the answer to that question has been a clear 'yes'.

I can remember to this day a defining moment in my life that tattooed a label on to my very mind. I was 12 years old and in year 8 at school. It was a maths lesson. The teacher had an unhelpful relationship with alcohol and we could often see a bottle sticking out of his bag. He had clearly had a few drinks that particular morning as he decided to read out everyone's scores from the latest maths test. He went through the register of names and informed us all of each pupil's scores: 'Tony, 85 per cent; Jane, 72 per cent; Rachel, 91 per cent; Graham, 74 per cent . . .' As my name approached, he stopped and said, 'Listen up, everyone. I can't believe it.' He giggled and spluttered out, 'Neil, 2 per cent.' His giggles turned into hysterical laughter, and the entire class joined in for what felt like an age. I remember feeling distinctly humiliated, small and obviously very dumb! What was the matter with me? Two per cent – I must be so stupid.

From then on, throughout my school life, I held a belief that I could not learn, so I simply stopped trying. It wasn't until I was much older, when I was diagnosed as having attention deficit disorder (ADD), that some of my challenges at school began to make more sense.

However, in a sense I swapped one label that had been imprinted on to my mind – the word 'dumb' – for another label that reads 'ADD'. Neither of those labels really defines me or gives me value, but both have stuck. I have used one to try and cancel out the other.

We all carry labels. Some, though, are big and make for a continual narrative that steers both the beliefs we hold about ourselves and the way in which we respond to people or situations.

For a long period of time I felt intimidated around academics and teachers. My mind would turn to jelly and I would splutter out nonsense whenever I was in the presence of someone I considered to be bright, because my brain said, 'You are stupid, you can only get 2 per cent. People will recognize very quickly that you are not bright!'

As Jesus passes us the soap to help to remove the sticky labels attached to our lives, he wants to address each of the labels, especially those of rejection, guilt and shame, with his own phrases.

Loved. He looks at you and says, 'I have loved you with an everlasting love,' and, as he gazes at you, he whispers, 'You are mine.'

Valued. He raises his hand to show you that on his palm he has written your name (see Isaiah 49.16). You are wanted and cared for; you belong to him.

Clean. To the things in life that fill you with horror, the memories of major failure and guilt, he says, 'Let's clear this up – you are forgiven.'

These things are far easier said than truly believed.

I carry a card around in my wallet, on which I have written a Bible passage, Exodus 14.13–14, with one change: I have inserted

WHAT LABELS DO YOU LIVE WITH OR HAVE YOU LIVED WITH?

DESCRIBE WHAT THAT LABEL LOOKS LIKE AND WHETHER YOU STILL CARRY IT.

REJECTION

_____
_____
_____
_____
_____

GUILT

_____
_____
_____
_____
_____

my own name into that verse. When I read it, it immediately becomes personal. I don't just read it. I recite it to myself, and I own it.

My mind developed a negative 'go to' narrative. It was formed in that maths lesson at the age of 12 and in part even before then, when I was five years old and had to have speech lessons for slurring my words because I couldn't breathe properly. The narrative states, 'You are worthless.' Theoretically I know that is not true. I am told that is not true by Christians, books and the Bible, and I have a family who reinforce by their behaviour towards me that I matter. However, when those thoughts intrude and gain momentum, I need to take control over that voice. When this happens the card comes out of my wallet and I read it over and over and over, until I have replaced that negative voice with a different one. I have to choose to believe what the card says even when an inner voice is shouting something else. Years later, I very rarely look at that card now – I have worked hard through words of truth to change the way my mind processes.

We have already looked at what Paul said in Romans 12 about being transformed by the renewing of our minds, but how do we do that? The answer comes again from Paul, in Philippians 4.8, to think on things that are true, noble, right, pure, lovely and admirable. We need to rewire our thinking by replacing negative thoughts with positive ones based on truth and hope.

What are some of the things you need to cancel out with words of truth? What are the labels that are stuck to you, and are so embedded that when you try to peal them off only the surface rips off and the label remains, a clear messy stain?

Deeply held issues can be resolved in a flash by the Holy Spirit, but more often than not that isn't the case and we have to choose to believe that lies are lies and need replacing by truths. That takes time, and it requires that we form habits of speaking truth over ourselves.

We also have to recognize that when labels are removed, circumstances can cause us to stick them right back on again. The label may have gone but the sticky residue from the glue can remain, and when prodded by an event or words spoken by others we put that label right back where the last one had been washed off over time by the soap of God's truth.

My encouragement to you is simple, but very difficult to follow – believe me, I know. Keep going, keep cancelling out the lies with

FINALLY, BROTHERS AND SISTERS,
WHATEVER IS

TRUE,

WHATEVER IS

NOBLE,

WHATEVER IS

RIGHT,

WHATEVER IS

PURE,

WHATEVER IS

LOVELY,

WHATEVER IS
ADMIRABLE
– IF ANYTHING IS
EXCELLENT OR
PRAISEWORTHY
– THINK ABOUT SUCH THINGS.
(PHIL. 4.8, NIV)

truth, erasing the negative experiences with hope, and when the spiralling poor thoughts crash inwards, causing doubt or anxiety, choose to speak new words of truth over and over and over.

It may be that your experiences and narrative are just too difficult to work through on your own. Be courageous and share them with someone you trust, and be willing to seek out professional help with a counsellor or even a doctor if need be. You matter too much to allow such negative thoughts to hold you captive.

Jesus offers freedom, and part of this freedom is receiving and living in our new narrative of being loved, valued and forgiven, and with a future filled with hope for this life and the next.

So what are the words, situations and past issues that have gripped you? Did you identify them earlier? Your very first step to living in truth is understanding what has a hold on you and blocks the freedom God has for you.

The rest of this chapter contains verses from God's word that you can use to replace negative narratives with words of hope and truth over your life. Memorize the verses and the points of truth if they are helpful to you. Consider repeating them over and over when doubts about who you are flood into your mind.

Has the time come to replace negative

thoughts with thoughts of hope and truth? Be both persistent and relentless in your pursuit of creating a new narrative and removing an old narrative that has taken deep root. It can be done. Be honest about the thoughts, but then allow a continual stream of new thoughts to wash over the old.

Narrative: 'I have failed and God can never forgive me.'
God's word of truth for you: 'There is now no condemnation for *me* [or write your name] because *I am* [or write 'he/she is'] in Christ Jesus' (Rom. 8.1).
Points of truth to recite: 'God knows my past; he loves me regardless; I am forgiven because of Jesus; my past does not have a hold on me any more.'

Narrative: 'I am worthless.'
God's word of truth for you: 'You created my inmost being; you knit me together in my mother's womb. I praise you because I am fearfully and wonderfully made' (Ps. 139.13–14, NIV).
Points of truth to recite: 'I am not a mistake; I was personally created by God; he considers me to be wonderfully made; I matter deeply to him.'

Narrative: 'I am repulsive.'
God's word of truth for you: '[Your name,] you are altogether beautiful, my love, there is no flaw in you' (Song of Sol. 4.7, ESV).
Points of truth to recite: 'I am created by God; I am beautiful to him; I am therefore loveable.'

Narrative: 'I am afraid.'
God's word of truth for you: '[Your name,] don't be afraid. Just stand still and watch the LORD rescue you today. The Egyptians [replace with your issue of fear] you see today will never be seen again. The LORD himself will fight for you. Just stay calm' (Exod. 14.13–14, NLT).

Points of truth to recite: 'God is aware; he promises to fight for me; nothing can stand against God; I will be okay.'

Narrative: 'I am anxious.'
God's word of truth for you: '[Your name,] do not be anxious about anything, but in every situation, by prayer and petition, with thanksgiving, present your requests to God. And the peace of God, which transcends all understanding, will guard your hearts and minds in Christ Jesus' (Phil. 4.6–7, NIV).
Points of truth to recite: 'I have no reason to be anxious; God promises to hear my requests and to give me peace; he is faithful and he is with me.'

Narrative: 'I will fail.'
God's word of truth for you: '[Your name,] I am the LORD your God who takes hold of your right hand and says to you, Do not fear; I will help you' (Isa. 41.13, NIV).
Points of truth to recite: 'God knows my abilities; he knows what I am facing; he promises to be with me and to help me; I do not need to be afraid.'

Narrative: 'I will be abandoned and rejected.'
God's word of truth for you: '[Your name,] the LORD himself will lead you and be with you. He will not fail you or abandon you, so do not lose courage or be afraid' (Deut. 31.8, GNB).

Points of truth to recite: 'God knows everything about me; he promises to lead me; he won't ever leave or abandon me; it will be okay.'

Narrative: 'I am going to get found out.'
God's word of truth for you: 'You have searched me, LORD, and you know me. You know when I sit down and when I rise; you perceive my thought from afar. You discern my going out and my lying down; you are familiar with all my ways' (Ps. 139.1–3, NIV).
Points of truth to recite: 'God knows everything about me already; there is nothing I can hide from him and yet he still loves and accepts me; I have nothing to hide or fear.'

Narrative: 'Everyone knows my issues.'
God's word of truth for you: '[Your name,] fear not, for you will not be put to shame; and do not feel humiliated, for you will not be disgraced; but you will forget the shame of your youth' (Isa. 54.4, NASB).
Points of truth to recite: 'While others may have mocked, God does not; I am loved and valued by him; my past will not define me; God creates my future.'

Narrative: 'I am not good enough.'
God's word of truth for you: '[Your name, be] confident of this very thing, that he who began a good work in you will complete it until the day of Jesus Christ' (Phil. 1.6, WEB).
Point of truth to recite: 'God designed me; he is working in and through me; he has not finished with me; I will achieve so much because of him.'

11 BEDROOM

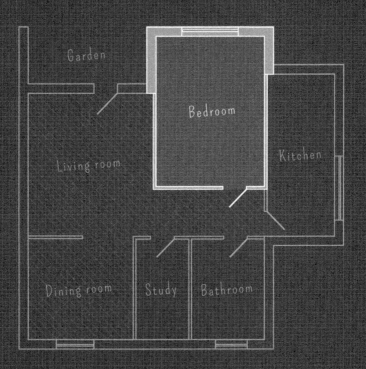

Garden

Bedroom

Kitchen

Living room

Dining room   Study   Bathroom

The bedroom of our lives is the place of privacy. It is our space, and therefore sacred, a zone where we can escape and be alone, where our thoughts are private and our activities go unscrutinized. It is our safe environment and one where people should knock before they enter, if indeed we let them in at all. What we do behind closed doors in this room is our business.

So far we have given Jesus access to the living room, dining room, kitchen, study and bathroom. He has also inspected the door, windows, walls, roof and foundations of the house. It would seem reasonable to have one place where even Jesus needs to knock.

However, it doesn't work that way. If we are going to make changes and to live as followers of Jesus, he requires an all-access pass. Nowhere is off-limits and furthermore, he wants the freedom to roam anywhere he likes once he has been allowed inside our house. He wants to see us for who we are and he is committed to working on those much-needed areas of change.

So, what does the bedroom represent?

Sleep? Homework? Private relationships? Sex? If it happens in this room he wants to know about it. Yes, even sex.

What this room really represents is something much deeper. This room asks, 'Who are we when no one is looking?' What do we do, what do we get up to, how does our behaviour differ, and what do we try to keep hidden and secret?

This room explores the real and authentic you. It is often in private that character is really formed, nurtured and developed.

WHO AM I...

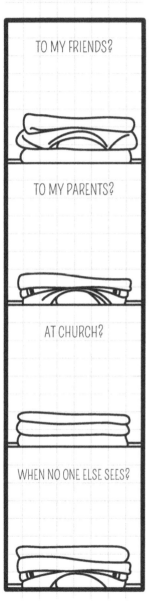

TO MY FRIENDS?

TO MY PARENTS?

AT CHURCH?

WHEN NO ONE ELSE SEES?

A friend of mine who is a social worker told me of a 16-year-old girl who was pregnant and wanted to keep the baby. The social worker asked if she knew who the father was. She didn't. The next question concerned how many sexual partners she might have had. She replied that she had slept with six people in her life. The social worker then asked how many partners she had slept with around the period in which she most likely got pregnant. Her answer was six! When pressed further it turned out that the girl had slept with all six guys on the same night at a party. She waited for one to finish, turfed him out and then found another. None of the guys was aware that she was moving from one person to another. Character was being formed in secret that night, which left her pregnant, with six potential teenage fathers.

Perhaps most people wouldn't act in that way, but all of us, left to our own devices, unsupervised and in the belief no one else will find out, will discover, when we are given an opportunity to meet a need, that we are opening the door to potentially poor decisions and allowing character to form in an unhelpful manner.

I remember a time at school when I had to do an exam. I had been sick the week before when everyone in my class had taken it. The teacher put me in a room, unsupervised. As I worked my way through the test, I couldn't remember anything of what I had previously learned. My backpack was in the corner and it just so happened to contain my notes from this class. I crept across the room, pulled out the notebook and used it as a reference for the test. The opportunity presented itself, I was unsupervised, and I cheated. I was convinced I would not be found out. I wasn't found out – in fact this is the first time I have shared the story. I suspect the reason I wasn't found out (other than that no one walked in on me) was because I failed the test! My own notes were incorrect. That, however, does not make my actions that day okay. I cheated.

Jesus is just as interested in who we are in private as in who we might be in public.

My observation is that we will always want to indulge our private character at the expense of our public character until we are truly satisfied in God. The reality is that we will never really be satisfied with who we are in private *or* public until we have enough of God in our lives. We will always want more, and give way to more temptations, until the 'more' in our lives is Jesus. However, I have also come to realize that we can reach a place where we know what it is like to be satisfied in Jesus – only then to discover that we leak. If we don't keep on seeking God, within a short period of time we will start finding alternatives to God, and that searching will take place in our private thoughts and spaces – even if we are passionately committed followers of Jesus!

My real point is this: the bedroom is perhaps the most dangerous place in your life. If it were just a place to sleep and rest then that would be one thing, but it is so much more. It really represents the you when no one else is watching. So who is that person?

When Jesus walks into this room, what does he see?

In Chapter 3 (Windows), we explored how we naturally want to cover things up and hide things because of shame. There may be aspects that are hidden in your private life (bedroom) that relate to shame. However, there may well be things that are hidden because

EVERYONE WHO
DOES EVIL HATES THE

LIGHT,

AND WILL NOT COME
INTO THE LIGHT
FOR FEAR THAT
THEIR DEEDS WILL BE

EXPOSED.

(JOHN 3.20, NIV)

you are feeding a desire or a need that is possibly unhelpful or unhealthy.

The Bible reminds us that people who do unhelpful or unhealthy things like to avoid the light for fear of being found out (John 3.20). Are there things in your life that you currently do that you would prefer people didn't know about?

Our bedroom may well symbolize habits that have developed and that we feed. This creates patterns that are either difficult to break or we do not want to break.

It might be that we watch movies or TV series that turn us on, and despite the tug on our conscience we just have to watch them. Or perhaps behind closed doors things have gone well beyond hugs with our girlfriend or boyfriend and the cycle can't be broken. It might be that we use cheat sites for homework essays, or we are chatting to our friends into the early hours when our parents have no idea. I don't know what the issue could be or how it looks, but whatever it is, it goes by unobserved and without scrutiny. This room presents you with the freedom to feed a desire that deep down you know is not right.

There have been times in my own life when things have been allowed to grow unchecked because I hadn't realized how subtle they were.

When something is allowed to grow, it can take time for us to realize that something seemingly innocent is actually a fully grown weed with deep roots. That weed doesn't want to be pulled out. What it really wants is to be watered all the more.

The only way to deal with a weed is to pull it out, but on your own that can be very hard. A weedkiller is far more effective, and that weedkiller is usually someone else.

Okay, so that sounds scary. Before you switch off and move to the next chapter because the thought of telling someone is so overwhelming that you just couldn't do it, work through this with me.

One of the toughest things I have ever had to do is bring someone up to speed on a challenge in my life. I expected to face judgement and hostility, but instead I was greeted with a hug, kindness and understanding. I left feeling so much better. The question you may need to answer is, 'What is the worst that could happen?' Then you need to ask, 'How serious am I about change?'

In most cases you will be surprised by the response you receive when you are open about your challenges. The Bible says that those who open up will receive compassion (Prov. 28.13).

In order for change to become a reality we need three things to take place (I use the acronym DAW to help me remember them). We need to be:

- Dissatisfied with our current situation;
- Aware of a better situation;
- Willing to take the first step.

What are the things in your private life that are hidden – the things you know that Jesus would be very interested in, and the things that would cause you stress if he started to rummage around inside you?

We don't need to think about it for long. We already know. Furthermore, Jesus already knows as well.

The writer of Psalm 44 realized that we can't hide anything from God, because he already knows what we do:

IN YOUR OWN LIFE, WHAT NEEDS TO COME INTO THE LIGHT?

DRINK/DRUGS
RELATIONSHIPS
OTHER
SOCIAL
MEDIA
GAMING
EXCESSIVE
STUDY
BINGE
WATCHING
PORN

If we had forgotten the name of our
God
or spread out our hands to a
foreign god,
would not God have discovered it,
since he knows the secrets of the
heart?
(Ps. 44.20–21)

Do you have weeds that have taken root in your life? Do they leave you feeling uneasy, or at least recognizing things need to change?

Once we reach the point of realizing that things are not right, and change is needed, we need to know what that change could look like. To do that we need to ask what freedom looks like.

If I have an obsession with porn, the solution isn't simply a question of removing porn from my life (though that is certainly an important step). It also means replacing it with something far more healthy and positive.

Reward yourself for breaking a habit by replacing it with a healthy habit or an activity with healthy routines and boundaries. This means something that you enjoy but that won't create problems for you. It may be going to the gym, taking up a new sport, subscribing to something you are really interested in, starting a new hobby or updating an existing one. It may also be about pushing yourself to be more social, to

DO YOU HAVE A WEED GROWING IN YOUR LIFE
THAT NO ONE KNOWS ABOUT?

_____

_____

_____

_____

_____

WHAT STAGE IS YOUR WEED AT?
☐ BARELY AWARE
☐ SHOOTS ARE PUSHING TO THE SURFACE
☐ AN UNDENIABLE WEED
☐ THE WEED HAS ROOTS SO DEEP THEY CAN'T
    BE REMOVED

IF YOU COULD ASK SOMEONE TO HELP YOU WHO
WOULD YOU ASK?

_____

_____

WHAT MIGHT HE OR SHE DO THAT COULD HELP?

_____

_____

_____

_____

_____

engage with friends and commit to activities. It could be pushing yourself to be more involved at church. I couldn't say what it might be for you, but the point is to replace the void with something that brings life.

In order to break free, you need first to be aware of the problem. Name it. Once you have named it, you need to want to change. Are you dissatisfied with living like this and doing

WHEN WERE YOU LAST
DISSATISFIED?

WERE YOU
AWARE
OF HOW THE SITUATION
COULD BE IMPROVED?

DID YOU TAKE THE
FIRST STEPS?

something that is unhealthy for you? If you are, then you need to stop whatever it is, by bringing what is in secret into the light and telling someone. Bring accountability to it. Let a friend, or mentor, help you to deal with it, even if it is a case of saying, 'I have been doing . . . and I want to stop doing it. I can't do that on my own. Will you keep checking in with me by asking me about it?'

Just knowing someone will ask you may be all that is required. However, if it is an addiction that you just can't break, it may take more than that. You may need to hand over your devices or ask someone to go to a clinic with you. It may be tough, but breaking habits requires tough action. People will love and support you throughout. Why? Because, in the words of Jesus, 'He that is without sin may throw the first stone' (John 8.7, my version). We are all fragile, broken people working through the challenges of life. Some are simply further along than others on the journey of wholeness, but no one is immune to cracks and failure. We have all messed up and we are all prone to making mistakes again.

Ultimately you need to remove from your life whatever it is that causes you to feed unhelpful and unhealthy habits. Only you know what that means, and, if you aren't sure, again ask someone who cares for you. Freedom is for the taking but it requires bringing things into the light. Jesus is in the light and the closer we are to him the harder it is for us to keep things in the dark.

Before we finish this chapter about the bedroom, which illustrates secrets that we willingly indulge in and habits that need to be broken, I want to touch on one object in the room in particular; namely the bed, because it often represents sex for us.

As Christians we believe that God has made us as sexual beings. Sex is a pleasure and a gift that God gives to relationships. We do, however, also believe that the gift of sex is to be enjoyed only within the boundaries of marriage. The Bible tells us that a man will unite with his wife and the two will become one.

Sex is more than a pleasurable experience or a procedure to start life (have babies). It is a powerful spiritual and emotional bond that takes two people and makes them one. They have connected in ways that God has intended for marriage alone.

If we sleep with many people, we are uniting and then ripping up the bond in ways that were never intended. The sacred (yes, I know it's a spiritual word, but it is sacred) act of sex is being misused and it is likely to create problems later on in life.

While statistically most people are not virgins on their wedding day, those who are are far more likely to remain together through the course of their lives and and to stay sexually faithful to each other than those who have had sex before marriage.

What is sex? Sex is more than two sexual organs. Sex goes beyond nakedness and intercourse. You are a sexual being, you were created for sex, but God desires that sex be an innocent experience between two people in the context of marriage, to strengthen the relationship and to protect each other with the knowledge that they have committed themselves only to each other.

What if you have had sex? What if you are sleeping with or doing stuff with your girl- or boyfriend now and until this point had not realized there was anything wrong with it? Even if you did know that

WHO DO YOU
TRUST?

ARE THEY
PERFECT?

WHY DO YOU
TRUST THEM?

ARE YOU WILLING TO TELL THEM
YOUR STRUGGLES?

Christians believe you should wait, you just couldn't. What do you do now?

First, we need to recognize that while God's best is for sex within marriage, God always forgives, and the reset button can be pressed. If you stop having sex, take your past experiences to God and are honest with whoever you go on to marry, then sex from any previous encounters will have no reason to spoil the bond in any way, shape or form that God has for you and your future spouse.

Second, you need to talk to whoever you are sleeping with or having sexual experiences with and tell them clearly why you don't believe you should continue, and then create boundaries from temptation. Probably keeping out of your bedroom and not being in the house alone will be a good start. Be aware of two other things – how quickly you get turned on from kissing, and what you watch, because if you are watching stuff that turns you on then your desire for sex will only increase.

Third, and this one will be tough, consider telling someone in your life who will hold you to account, by being honest and asking that they check in with you about how things are going.

God wants the best for us and he wants us to have the very best relationships. But one relationship stands out far and above any other, and that is the one with our future spouse. That relationship is one that you commit to for the rest of your life. He or she will be your soulmate and your very best friend. Protect that relationship now by holding off from sexual experiences with other people and waiting until the day of your marriage.

At the heart of everything is one overriding relationship, and that is our relationship with God. The more we allow Jesus to have full access to every room in our lives, giving him the freedom to make changes, and push into a deeper and more satisfying relationship with him, the less we will be tempted to keep things in the dark and the more comfortable we will be about the powerful transformation to come. Jesus wants to help you become more and more like him, and to become more and more like the very best person God created you to be!

12 GARDEN

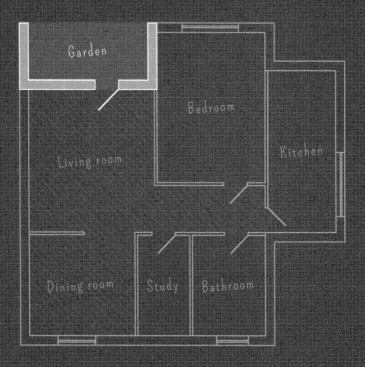

Garden

Bedroom

Kitchen

Living room

Dining room

Study

Bathroom

Our garden is an absolute mess. Our fence recently blew over and hit the neighbour's car; there are weeds everywhere and our puppy just keeps digging large holes for us to fall into. But, I keep looking at my garden and dreaming of what it could become. In fact, it has so much natural potential that I can't help getting excited. As you will have gathered, I am not a gardening nerd, but this garden could become something extraordinary with just a little tender loving care.

And so could you – I mean this – even though you are already amazing!

Jesus has been walking around every room in your house, and the journey of transformation is clearly underway, but the garden – well, the garden is for the world to see all the potential and beauty that can be found within it.

The garden represents your impact on the world. What grows in the garden could really make a big difference.

When we lived in Thailand as a family, our garden had 12 different fruit trees. We had so much fresh and juicy fruit that we couldn't eat it all – we shared its abundance with people all around.

That is what the garden is for. It's a metaphor for that aspect of your life that you share with the world. It can be such a powerful blessing.

After nearly 18 years of living overseas, when we had finally returned to the UK, we were back at the airport within less than four weeks and having to say goodbye to our son, Jake.

> 'I AM THE
> **TRUE VINE,**
> AND MY FATHER IS THE
> **GARDENER.**
> HE CUTS OFF EVERY BRANCH
> IN ME THAT BEARS NO FRUIT,
> WHILE EVERY BRANCH THAT
> DOES BEAR FRUIT HE PRUNES
> SO THAT IT WILL BE EVEN MORE
> **FRUITFUL.**
> YOU ARE ALREADY CLEAN
> BECAUSE OF THE WORD I
> HAVE SPOKEN TO YOU.
> **REMAIN IN ME,**
> AS I ALSO REMAIN IN YOU.
> NO BRANCH CAN BEAR
> **FRUIT**
> BY ITSELF; IT MUST REMAIN
> IN THE VINE. NEITHER CAN
> YOU BEAR FRUIT UNLESS
> YOU REMAIN IN ME.
>
> **'I AM**
> **THE VINE;**
> YOU ARE THE BRANCHES.
> IF YOU REMAIN IN ME AND I IN
> YOU, YOU WILL BEAR MUCH
> **FRUIT;**
> APART FROM ME YOU
> CAN DO NOTHING.'
> **(JOHN 15.1–5, NIV)**

Jake was leaving for the USA where he was going to attend university. The family clung to him. One by one, each of us said goodbye to him, and I have to tell you there were plenty of tears. When my turn came, I hugged him, pulled him in really close and whispered, 'Jake, if you forget everything I've ever taught or shown you then remember this one thing!' I then went on to tell him what I wanted him to remember. And then I let go, and within a few moments he was out of sight and gone.

I think Jesus had a similar moment with his disciples, just after the Last Supper. He headed towards the garden of Gethsemane where he prayed and was then arrested. He had precious few moments left with his followers. I suspect that the walk was a heavy one for him, knowing what was to come and knowing that things would never be the same again with his disciples. Like that moment that I had with Jake, I think Jesus also had one with his disciples as he passed through the vineyard. If they were to forget everything else, then they needed to remember this one thing.

> 'Hey everyone, come here, gather round!' I imagine the disciples to be like wild cats, constantly moving. 'Matthew, John, come here for a moment . . Thomas, stop questioning everything Peter says and quieten down for just a moment.'

Once he has their attention, he points to a vine.

'Guys, my Father is the gardener, and I am the vine.'

In case that seems a bit abstract, he continues to unpack the metaphor.

'You are the branches that connect to the vine. Do you get it?'

I suspect a few puzzled faces and vague nods were exchanged.

'A branch that connects to the vine will be strong, because the vine gives valuable life to the branch, and the branch then produces grapes, incredible grapes!'

Still blank expressions.

'If you remain connected to me, you will produce fruit in your life. If you are not connected to me then you won't – just like a branch that is not connected to the vine and so has no life source, it just shrivels up and dies. But from me comes life.'

For a more accurate account you will be better off reading John 15.1–5. However, the point is simple: Jesus gives life to us; he is our power source, and that power has an impact on us and the world around us.

Our garden is a picture of the fruit that comes from being connected to Jesus. The more we allow Jesus to make his powerful changes in us, the more the world will see the difference Jesus makes. Continuing the metaphor, more fruit will be available for picking.

How do we remain connected to Jesus?

The first step is to let him into our lives. That happened when we became a Christian. The next step is to give him total access to every area of our lives – an all-access pass that must not expire. This is what almost every page of this book has attempted to explore with you. The third step is to ensure we have a strong and active connection to him. We do this by prayer, worship, reading our Bible and books that help us to process and grow, and by belonging to a church and an active Christian youth group. That's a lot! However, the more

DRAW A DOOR

TO ILLUSTRATE WHETHER YOU'RE AN OPEN OR CLOSED PERSON.

you work at the garden of your life, the more will grow in that garden. To be more precise, the more you allow God to work in the garden of your life – and you continue to play your part – the more connected you will become and the more the world around will see Jesus in you.

I have a few final thoughts before we reach the end of this book. The first thing is: pull down your fence. Mine blew away, but the gardens of our lives shouldn't have barriers to the world around us.

Don't always be private. Be open, be kind and engage with people in your life. Let them see your garden (who you are) and let them pick the fruit that gives life.

Second, live an intentional life. Intentionally grow the right things in your garden and let people see what is growing. What does that mean?

I attended sports college after leaving school. To get in, you had to perform at county level. Having been ranked number three in the nation and having fought for Yorkshire at karate, I ticked that box. My class was full of very gifted athletes. I was good at punching and kicking and precious little else, whereas many of the others were outstanding in pretty much anything on which they focused.

To the best of my knowledge I was the only Christian on campus. If there were other Christians I didn't find them, and I looked pretty hard. My classmates lived pretty raw lives: they would come in each day and share what they'd done the night before – how drunk they got, what drugs they took, or who they had managed to sleep with. Anything that came out of their mouths was fairly colourful and definitely not grandma-appropriate.

One day, in a particular class, the lecturer said that he wanted everyone to give a presentation on any leisure industry of interest in the UK. That was very vague and open to interpretation as to what it could include. What I think he really meant was, 'Speak on your sports background', but he didn't say that. He said 'any'. The real mistake he made was not checking what each person would present.

The first person got up and he was a tennis player He spoke about the tennis industry in the UK. He was good, and connected well. The second person was a sprinter and she spoke on the athletic industry; she was engaging. My moment came and everybody expected me to speak on martial arts. I should have, but I didn't.

My youth leader had told me that the Bible says, 'Always be prepared to give an account of your faith.' It seemed like such a moment.

I got up and said, 'Let me tell you about a leisure industry that not many of you may have considered to be recreational. Every week over 10 per cent of people, which by the way is far more than the number of people who go to football matches, attend church. Yes, church . . . so let me tell you about church.' I proceeded to paint a brief picture of a church service – songs, prayers, readings and then the sermon. 'Each week someone will preach, so I thought I would give you a sample of what a church sermon is like . . .' I then spent the remainder of my presentation preaching to my class.

In my mind I imagined everyone becoming a Christian there and then. I had not anticipated it resembling more a car crash than a repentance meeting. However, by the end, every head was down, not out of reverent prayer or the conviction of sin, but out of complete awkward embarrassment. Nobody looked up, and in the break

LIST FIVE THINGS THAT
MAKE YOU DIFFERENT:

1

2

3

4

5

MARK EACH DIFFERENCE WITH A

√ OR ✗

DEPENDING ON WHETHER
YOU'RE HAPPY WITH
THAT DIFFERENCE.

everybody avoided me. I had massively misjudged my moment.

I remember going home that day on my own, and saying, 'Okay, God, I gave this preaching deal a go and it didn't work. I am never preaching again! So here is the deal. I will go to church, pray every day, read my Bible, go to youth group and have an accountability buddy, but I am not telling anybody about you again!'

I kept to my word. I did exactly that.

During my very last week at college, I was walking down the corridor and a group of my classmates were in a huddle. As I passed them by they called back, 'Hey Neil, we were just talking about you.'

I didn't know how to respond. What were they saying?

'Oh yeah?'

'Yeah, we were saying that you are different!'

Different? When I use the word different, I don't usually mean it in a positive way. When I eat at someone else's house and they ask, 'How was the food?' I might say, 'That was different.' What I really mean is, 'That was horrible!' 'Different' covers up how you might feel.

'Different – how?'

'Well, you never get drunk, take drugs, sleep around; you never talk about people badly, you don't tell rude jokes and you don't swear . . . you are different!'

I didn't know if the list of nevers and don'ts was a good or bad thing. I just waited for him to continue.

'So, yeah, you are different, but we really like you, you are cool! However, we want to know what makes you different.'

And there it was – I had preached my heart out to my entire class and nobody listened to a word I said, but I lived as a follower of Jesus and everyone wanted to know what made me different.

I was able gently to share my faith, which resulted in a classmate walking out of her way home that night to ask me question after question about God and who he was and whether he really loved her.

Preaching has its place, but not usually in a class lecture. However, living as a follower of Jesus for the world to see is an absolute must.

The Bible refers to a follower of Jesus as a disciple. The word 'disciple' when translated into English most closely relates to the word 'apprentice'.

An apprentice is someone learning a trade or a skill.

The very first reference to people who followed Jesus in the book of Acts was not as 'Christians' but as 'people of the way'. Therefore, a disciple is simply someone who is learning the ways of Jesus.

As you allow Jesus to make more and more profound changes in each room and area of your house (life), you will become more like him. The most effective way to become like Jesus and to learn to be like him is by spending time in his presence, with others who also follow him, and studying what it means to be like Jesus.

The more you do that, the more people will start to notice there is something very different about you, but different in this case does not mean bad!

So, should we tell people about Jesus, or just let them figure it out? Yes and yes.

Your friends may not appreciate you preaching at them, but you don't need to. For example, on Monday morning, the conversation goes something like this: 'What did you do over the weekend?'

WHICH OF YOUR FRIENDS...

SEEM CLOSED TO SPIRITUAL STUFF?

GO TO CHURCH?

ARE COMFORTABLE WITH YOUR FAITH?

TALK ABOUT GOD WITH YOU?

'Not much. I hung out with friends, watched Netflix and went to church.'

Then move on to the next subject, but don't for a minute think they didn't catch the fact you threw in the word 'church'. Just don't linger there; it probably isn't the time to repeat the pastor's sermon for them all to hear (I am not sure there is ever a time for that).

When something is shared that is tough, just drop in again, 'I am really sorry. I will absolutely pray for you about that', and then move on to the next subject.

If the word 'church' caught their attention, then 'pray for you' is a spiritual explosive that you can bet has caused internal reactions. What's more, you can come back to the subject at a later time: 'Hey, so I said I would pray for X – what happened?'

If your friends are not yet pushing you on some of the things you have been saying, it is not a problem. Just keep it natural.

Keep dropping in aspects of your life and faith that matter and are relevant, but don't stay there. When they are stressed about exams, let them know how you deal with stress – it might be in prayer or a sense of peace you get by trusting Jesus or from reading certain verses in the Bible.

The secret is to find ways to connect, but don't make it heavy. Then, over time, when you know they are comfortable with the fact you have a faith, move to questions (avoid statements – people react better to questions):

- 'Have you ever gone to church? What was it like?'
- 'Do you ever pray? Do you think someone is listening?'
- 'How do you handle stress?'
- 'Do you ever think about God?'
- 'What do you believe?'
- 'How do you get through tough times?'

This list isn't exhaustive, and perhaps none of the above questions are right for your friends at this point. Work out for yourself what questions matter to you and to your friends. And listen to the answers: this is about going deeper, not about demonstrating your knowledge.

The more questions you ask, the more you will learn about your friends, and the more you will discover where they are at on the journey of faith and belief. However, pace the questions to their willingness to engage. Give them too much at once and they may not be interested in more at a later time.

Remember this: everyone is spiritual, but not everyone realizes it or believes that the answer can be found in God. And that is okay – we are called to journey and live life with them. They may never believe, but what matters is that you remain an authentic and real friend regardless, even if God is taken off the agenda.

Finally, be sure to step outside your garden and help other people with theirs. We live in a very selfish world, a world of 'me' and 'I'. What does it look like for you to push yourself to help people when there is no benefit in doing so?

We are called to help change this world. That will always come at a cost. It may or may not result in other people coming to know Jesus. However, the world needs God's ambassadors to take care of other people in need, to fight for the environment, to be advocates for justice and to show mercy.

You have a role to play here. Take care of your garden, but get stuck into helping other people with theirs.

The great commandment is simply this: 'Love God and love others.' Loving others is loving God, but it could be hard to love God if we don't love others when he has specifically asked us to do just that.

Make a difference.

So let's finish where we started. Is your life as good as it gets?

The answer is 'no'. God's plan for you is so much greater than you can ever imagine. However, it requires a willingness to allow Jesus to have an all-access pass around your house, into every area of your life, and to make the changes needed within you; to work on the garden so the world can see the impact and connection to Jesus, and to move off your patch and help others who are in need.

God has a dangerously awesome plan for you. Let him work in you in such a way that you get to experience exactly what that means and how it looks.

Don't get bogged down with how you might view yourself. Remember, you are a child of God and deeply loved by him. Catch hold of the person God is preparing you to become, but, equally, don't get caught up in the future – live in the moment, recognizing that, though the renovation of your life is not complete, what Jesus is currently doing within you and through you is incredible.

Keep moving forward with him.

One last thought

WHERE DO YOU NEED TO BE GIVING MOST
ATTENTION AND ALLOWING JESUS TO SET TO
WORK IN YOUR LIFE?

WRITE DOWN IF YOU NEED TO TAKE ANY ACTION
IN EACH AREA OF YOUR LIFE:

FOUNDATIONS
FLOORBOARDS
ENSURING JESUS IS THE MAIN FOCUS IN OUR LIVES

_____
_____
_____
_____

FOUNDATIONS
WINDOWS
ENSURING THERE IS NOTHING HIDDEN, SO THAT
JESUS CAN DEAL WITH OUR GUILT AND SHAME

_____
_____
_____
_____

FOUNDATIONS
WALLS
ENSURING OUR IDENTITY AND IMAGE ARE VIEWED
THROUGH THE EYES OF JESUS RATHER THAN THE
EYES OF THE WORLD

_____
_____
_____
_____

FOUNDATIONS
ROOF
ENSURING THAT, WHEN THE STORMS OF LIFE
HIT US, WE ARE PROTECTED FROM THEIR
DEVASTATION BECAUSE OF OUR FAITH IN JESUS

_____
_____
_____
_____

INDIVIDUAL ROOMS
LIVING ROOM
ALLOWING JESUS TO HELP US FOCUS OUR REST
TIME ON THINGS THAT BRING LIFE AND HEALTH

_____
_____
_____
_____

INDIVIDUAL ROOMS
DINING ROOM
ALLOWING JESUS TO HELP US PRIORITIZE FAMILY
TIME AND RELATIONSHIPS AND ALLOW THAT
SPACE TO BE THE BEST THAT IT CAN POSSIBLY BE

_____
_____
_____
_____

INDIVIDUAL ROOMS
KITCHEN
ALLOWING JESUS TO HELP US EXPLORE WHAT
HEALTHY BOUNDARIES AND HABITS LOOK LIKE IN
OUR LIVES

_____

_____

_____

_____

INDIVIDUAL ROOMS
STUDY
ALLOWING JESUS TO HELP US TO DEVELOP A
LIFE-GIVING, FLEXIBLE AND POWERFUL
RELATIONSHIP WITH HIM

_____

_____

_____

_____

INDIVIDUAL ROOMS
BATHROOM
ALLOWING JESUS TO REMOVE THE DEEP AND
NEGATIVE TAGS THAT HAVE ATTACHED
THEMSELVES TO US

_____

_____

_____

_____

INDIVIDUAL ROOMS
BEDROOM
ALLOWING JESUS INTO THE PRIVATE AREAS OF
OUR LIVES THAT WE WISH TO KEEP HIDDEN AND
CLOSED

_____

_____

_____

_____

GARDEN AND WORLD
EXPLORING WITH JESUS HOW TO LIVE A LIFE ON
DISPLAY FOR THE WORLD AROUND

_____
_____
_____
_____

THE UNWRITTEN
CHAPTER
WHAT HAS THIS BOOK MISSED OUT THAT YOU
WISH TO GIVE JESUS AN ALL-ACCESS PASS TO?

_____
_____
_____
_____

YOUTH FOR CHRIST

We're all about seeing young people's lives changed by Jesus.

As part of a worldwide Christian movement, we passionately demonstrate the love of God, declare who Jesus is and encourage a decision to follow him and disciple young people to live their lives to the full.

We provide pioneering teams in local centres spread across the nation, original resources supplied to over 4500 churches and youth groups, leadership and evangelism training for young adults, and missional teams that tour the country. Through these, we are commissioned to be people who take the good news relevantly to every young person across Britain.

To remain relevant means that innovation comes as standard and we remain fully reliant on God for his inspiration, leadership and provision.

If you want to know more about Youth for Christ and the ways that you can partner with us, go to yfc.co.uk/underconstruction